P9-DTQ-895

DIARY OF A WILDERNESS DWELLER

Happy 77th Birthday

R.C.

love
mary Lou

1996.

DIARY OF A
WILDERNESS DWELLER

Chris Czajkowski

All My Best

Chris Czajkowski

ORCA BOOK PUBLISHERS

Copyright © 1996 Chris Czajkowski

No part of this publication may be reproduced, stored in a retrieval system, or transmitted, in any form or by any means, without the prior written permission of the publisher, except by a reviewer who may quote brief passages in review.

Canadian Cataloguing in Publication Data
Czajkowski, Chris, 1947 –
  Diary of a wilderness dweller

  ISBN 1-55143-059-2

1. Czajkowski, Chris, 1947 – 2. Coast Mountains (BC and Alaska)—
Biography. 3. Women—British Columbia—Biography. I. Title.
FC3845.C7Z49 1996 971.1'104'092 C96–910286–0
F1089.C7C93 1996

The publisher would like to acknowledge the ongoing financial support of The Canada Council, the British Columbia Ministry of Small Business, Tourism and Culture, and the Department of Canadian Heritage.

Cover design by Christine Toller
Cover photographs and interior illustrations by the author
Printed and bound in Canada

Orca Book Publishers
PO Box 5626, Station B
Victoria, BC V8R 6S4
Canada

Orca Book Publishers
PO Box 468
Custer, WA 98240-0468
USA

10 9 8 7 6 5 4 3 2 1

To my father
He would have loved it here

ACKNOWLEDGEMENTS

Thank you Gloria and Roger
And Bob and Francie
If you were not there
I would have to find someone else
For I would not be able to live in the wilderness
Alone

PROLOGUE

Through the skin of my clothes I feel the rock. It is a little rough, a little sharp in places, sunwarmed, lichen-stained, a non-descript granite. It is split and eroded, half-drowned in a tide of juniper and kinikinik which, competing for space and sunlight, are unwitting partners in the slow minuet of life. But limbs can extend only so far from the parent root, particularly in this harsh climate, and the rock is too large to be engulfed. Its freckled heart, which warms my back, lies open to the sky.

Were I to pull away the sprawling skirts of fir, the wind-bent pines, the straggling slide alder and mountain rhododendron that surround this or any other rock in the vicinity, or even dig deep enough among the mats of sedges, crowberries and soggy cushions of sphagnum mosses in the small swamp to the north of me, I would find no solid base, just more boulders with gaping holes between and still more rocks below. What created this chaos? The rocks lie in a valley, but it is a very shallow one, the edge of a plateau really, where the Chilcotin meets the eastern foothills of the Central Pacific Coast Range. The tops of the hills that define the valley are mere upthrust piles of boulders, just as broken as the floor; there seem to be no outcrops from which these rocks could have fallen. Presumably the ice arranged them thus 10,000 years ago, they that were once part of the wall of granite that rears, still ice-hung, to the west; and before that beneath the sea; and before that in the molten core of the earth, and before that part of some other rock in some other place (for I have read that the tectonic plates are constantly submerging and re-emerging.) But although these rocks are worn, they are still quite angular and appear to have succumbed more to wind, weather and the minute erodings of lichens than the over-powering grinding of the ice. They lie, bulge, rear, subside and tumble in every conceivable direction, even plunging into the darkening depths of the lake and rising again to form islands. They are loose, sometimes precariously balanced. They teeter as I walk on them and if I remove these, the ones beneath are no more solidly placed. There are holes and gaps beneath them, a network of airspaces which reaches into darkness. It would seem impossible that anything could grow here.

And yet, from a distance, the country seems clothed in an un-broken pelt of forest, generously spotted with large lakes. Something must have blocked the interstices between the rocks sufficiently to control the flow of water. There is a little coarse-grained soil visible in places, but most smaller plants grow in thin mats of duff and moss; they are easily uprooted. The trees, however, are extraordi-narily tough. The have to be to survive fiercely contrasting temperatures, thin air and the wind. Many spiral like watch springs or sport ground-hugging skirts of vegetation from which erupt bleached, weathered trunks a hundred years old but ramrod stiff and hard as iron. On some of these, a thin strip of bark still clings to the leeward side and from it sprouts an improbable piece of vegeta-tion, wizened and tortured beyond belief. Somehow roots have tapped the poor resources of the scant soil, they have penetrated cracks, avoided sterile cavities, run deep to find water, and have cov-ered all the land. They embrace the rocks: those trees which finally blow over have stones so solidly entrapped in their network of roots that boulders as big as a man's torso are wrenched far from the ground. These are new-skinned and pale, uncolonized as yet by li-chens, naked as a sparrow's egg. They may sit there for a century before the roots rot sufficiently to release them. The roots hold them like a badge: "We are long dead, but we still have power."

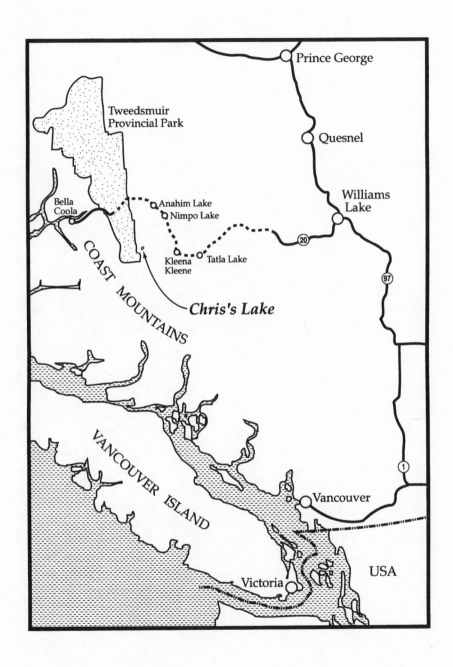

PART ONE

CHAPTER 1

June 26, 1988

It is two days since I left my truck at the end of a logging road twenty miles east of here. I have hiked through unmarked forest and over a mountain, through country I have never seen before, to reach a point of land jutting into an unnamed lake, five-thousand-feet high in the Coast Range of British Columbia. And yet, unbelievably, I now have rights, in the eyes of our civilization's laws, to adapt this uncompromising pile of boulders with its wind-weary trees to my own ends; I plan to build on it, single-handedly, two cabins, a business, and a life.

I must be crazy.

The reality, now that I am here with the object of staying, is a lot more daunting than the dream-image I have carried for so long in my mind. Gone are the rose-tinted spectacles of my first trip, when I came in from the coast in perfect, August-blue weather. Gone is the euphoria of the second visit, a similarly exciting adventure, when I snowshoed along a forty-mile trapper's trail from the interior. At that time I was on this rocky point for a grand total of three hours and had eyes for nothing but the huge, fantastic drifts and the four-foot-deep, fairy-tale covering of snow that smoothed and prettied the landscape and concealed a multitude of problems. Now, after a wearying, two-day scramble over a third and completely different route, through untracked bush and beset by flies, I see the rockpile for the gross impracticality that it really is. Ah romance, how glittery is your tinsel! How slyly you sugarcoat your pills.

You would think that I would have learned something from the first cabin I built, not forty miles from here along the Atnarko River.[1] There, I had flat ground, tall trees, and help to haul and lift the logs. Although the Atnarko location was, like this one, at the end of a long walk from nowhere, the route to it had already been established. Being 3,500 feet lower than here, the climate there was much kinder and, when the water was open, much of the journey could be travelled by canoe. But I have now launched myself at this unrealistic jumble of boulders and tortured trees, twenty miles from the nearest human being, and the enormity of what I have so casually undertaken is staring me in the face.

I became interested in the place by looking at a map. It was on the bottom right-hand corner of the same 1:50,000 sheet as the Atnarko cabin. Maps have always held a fascination for me. I read all manner of information into the tiny, implacable marks that cover the paper. Because the lake was both high and on the eastern side of British Columbia's Coast Range, I imagined it would be much drier and have a very different ecosystem to that of the semi-coastal Atnarko Valley. I figured that the point that jutted into the lake would have good exposure to sunlight and would probably have an excellent view of the main divide of the Coast Range. I did not know if it was possible to get to the lake directly from the Atnarko but, since I was living there, that would be the first route to try. There was a rough trail up river which would take care of the first day's travel, but this landed me in the wild, southern end of the Tweedsmuir Provincial Park, beyond which the country becomes increasingly rugged. The trail ended in a swamp after which there was the four-thousand-foot

---

[1] See *Cabin at Singing River.*

wall of the valley to negotiate, most of which was passable only to a goat. No one I knew had been that way; perhaps no human being ever had.

The swamp was horrendous, being full of creeks and bogholes and completely tangled with overhead brush and windfalls. But with the valley wall, I lucked out. I picked the most promising route, a spur alongside a deep-cut creek, and found a major game trail thick with fresh deer, bear, and moose tracks. Judging by the frequency of its use, it must have been the only route out of the valley for miles. In places the rocky steps were so large that my dog could not jump up them until I removed her pack. I had no idea that moose could be so agile.

Once over the top of the valley rim, the ground flattened out then sloped, very gently, towards the east. I was now at the marshy head of one of the many branches of Whitton Creek. It was not really a new watershed, for after running east for forty miles into Charlotte Lake, Whitton Creek curves back round and cascades through a wild cut in the Atnarko Valley wall back into the river not three miles above my old cabin.

The new country, as expected, was very different. The trees, mostly stunted pines and balsams, were sparsely clumped and interspersed with wide and frequent swampy meadows free of brush. Already, by late August, they were bronzed by frosts, great golden carpets of sedge and rush spangled with sky-blue pools and the slowly winding, ever-growing creek. Now that the forest had fallen back, I could see the mountains behind me and I was in no way disappointed. They reared shining and marble-white against the deep blue sky, permanently snow-covered, and dominated by twelve-thousand-foot Mt. Monarch, the highest mountain in Tweedsmuir Park. (Just, for the boundary runs through the middle of it.)

Despite its openness, the country was not all that easy to travel through because the meadows were boggy enough to make walking in them uncomfortable and, on dry ground, rock, windfall, and the tangled spreading skirts of the balsam fir were constant obstacles. The first foray into a new country always takes more time than subsequent trips, particularly as I followed every curve of the swelling creek which put more miles onto the journey than it might have. Thus it was two and a half days after leaving home before I finally stood on the shores of "my lake." It was, however, everything I had imagined: golden sun, blue water, white mountains, and the clean, fresh wind from the snows. But then nothing looks less than perfect under such conditions; had I hit a spell of foul weather I might have had a more realistic opinion about the place.

The machinations of the Land Office (or "Ministry of Lands and Housing" to give it its correct title) proved torturous. It seemed simple enough at first. I had to stake a claim, file it, and give a commercial reason for being there — the government was not going to process the application without a commitment from the licencee to try and make money out of it. This is somewhat ironic, for in fact it is impossible to make a living out of this country. Homesteading was out of the question in this high, rocky land with its short growing season. The area was worthless (I hoped) for logging and mining and, even if I was so inclined, the trap line was occupied. There was only one commercial reason that both I and the country were fit to undertake: tourism. Even that was limited here. The lake had a poor reputation for fishing; and the outfitting rights (that is, horseback riding and hunting) already belonged to someone else. But I did not, in any case, have the skills or temperament for those aspects of tourism. That left me with the foot travellers: the hikers, backpackers, artists, photographers, and naturalists, those who do not have to catch or kill something to feel fulfilled.

Staking a claim involved paying a $25 fee and completing, in triplicate, a *Notice of Intention to Apply for a Disposition of Crown Land.* There were immediate difficulties with the form. *"Here describe,"* it said, *"by giving name of lake, mountain, stream, village etc. in vicinity ..."* As far as I knew, the lake had no official name. The river appeared to be part of Whitton Creek, but there were several unnamed branches of the river, my lake being on one of the southern ones. The paper continued: *"Failing that, give directions from the nearest bit of surveyed land."* Well, that was twenty miles east on Charlotte Lake, the nearest place at which anything that could remotely be called a road arrived. So I gave the map reference and described the point as being northwest of the outlet of the third lake east of the park boundary on the next to southernmost branch of Whitton Creek, describing the claim as running two hundred metres northeast, then northwest, then southwest, and finally southeast to form a square *"from a post planted at least a metre above ground on the corner of the proposed property."* (I reckoned nature's planting would be good enough, and I used a tree at the tip of the point.) The two-hundred-metre measurements were the Land Office's stipulated minimums and, within that area, there appeared to be two good cabin sites, which is what I wanted. Two copies of this erudite document were to be sent into the Office, and the third was wrapped in a plastic bag and tied, with red flagging tape, to the tree on the end of the point. The Land Office retaliated fairly quickly with a demand for $100 filing fees and an intimation that my annual rent would be close to the minimum of $200 per year, and that the processing would take three months. That, said the Land Office, was all I would have to do.

But in three months' time, there was no word. Upon enquiry, they gave the first of several excuses I have since largely forgotten ("It is winter so we cannot fly in to inspect it" being one). This went on for a year and a half before the licence was finally (in triplicate) in my hands. It was not the simple document I had been led to believe. It was so heavily loaded in the government's favour that no one in their right mind would sign it. It was for only five years (hardly time to build the cabins, let alone establish a business) and there were clauses that meant that "the Owner" (i.e., the government) could, at any time it wished, grant the use of the same lease to anyone else who might want it for other purposes. (In other words, someone could log every tree in sight, open up a mine beneath my foundations, or set a trap in front of my door.) The Owner could also terminate the lease for no reason whatsoever and demand that I leave within sixty days: within that time, I would have to remove all trace of my occupancy — at my expense. Should a proper survey be required, the Owner was entitled to commandeer one, again at my expense, which, in this unsurveyed country accessible only by float plane, would amount to many thousands of dollars .

Also, the area for which I had applied had been considerably reduced, despite my having adhered to the government's own minimal measurements. When I queried this they told me I would thus be entitled to too much waterfront: the Land Office obviously envisions a future cottage suburbia here, à la Ontario, with rows of plots just wide enough to anchor a boat — I sincerely hope that I will never be witness to that. I had ended up with 0.3266 hectares, about a quarter of what I expected; that means the best cabin site is now unavailable to me. I wonder what sort of building experience is possessed by the people in the Land Office. Someone came and inspected it — I saw photos of it in the file when I went to the Office in Williams Lake. In a city you can manipulate any landscape with a machine, but here I will be using only very simple tools and be very much subject to whatever the land dictates. The Land Office, naturally, had protected itself by stating that it bore no responsibility if the lease was not suited to the purpose for which it had been applied.

Having originally expected that filing fees and rents were to be the only costs, I was now sprung with the need to show evidence of a million-dollar liability insurance policy — far more expensive than the rent — and to make a term deposit of $1,000 which I would forfeit at the termination of the lease if I did not return the land to the Owner in a suitable condition — whatever that may mean. To me $1,000 was an enormous sum, one for which I was totally unprepared. Do logging companies and mines pay a bond of the same amount? They, with their turnover of millions? Do they leave the land in a "suitable condition"?

As a business proposition, the whole thing was a disaster. I, as the licencee, had not a single legal leg to stand on. By placing my name on this document (in triplicate), I was proposing to spend every penny I owned and several years of my life on a grossly impractical heap of boulders with absolutely no guarantee of a future.

But I signed the lease. What else could I do?

The first route I had used to come here, from the Atnarko, is far too long to be practical. The trapper's trail, which I had used on the snowshoe trip, came in principally from the northeast. It would still be the best one for winter travel, as it stayed within the safety of the trees, but would be boggy and uninteresting in summer. The shortest route from the road to my lake (if a fifteen-mile, two-hour mud wallow deserves to be called a road) is a fairly direct hike of about twenty miles due west. This is the journey I have just completed. After the drive, there is a trail for the first five miles, but from then on I scrambled through brush and swamp along a creek named "Maydoe," (which is apparently an English distortion of the Carrier word meaning "white man.") The creek is strung with little lakes and very pretty, but the country beside them is either a tangle of spruce or a jungle of boulders; unless I can find a better route, I am going to have a great deal of work before anything close to a real trail exists.

The character of the country changed as I climbed into the mountains and left the dry, Chilcotin plateau behind. The swampy meadows were already hinting at their summer extravagance and beginning to bloom with paintbrush, arnica, and valerian. The little lakes were gems set in Japanese settings of rocks and twisted trees. The top lake was typical, a disc no more than three yards across. I camped beside it and planned my next day's hike up through the last vestiges of subalpine forest and the bald mountain slope beyond.

The wind, which had been gusty during the afternoon, rose to fiendish proportions during the night. The morning was wild, with rattling showers and brief flashes of rainbows.

I kept close to the tree line which ran diagonally up the mountainside. I plodded up over heath and crowberry and crossed splashing, flower-starred streams which gushed from disintegrating snow slabs. And then there was the sudden incomparable exhilaration of seeing over the top and into a new valley — my valley — on the other side. The land swooped steeply down to a long, banana-shaped lake below, then climbed a forested valley to a body of water shining in the middle distance. That was my lake, cradled in its high plateau, backed by an impressive array of the glacier-swathed Coast Range.

The wind hit me with a bang. "The Promised Land!" I shouted into it. The dog, who has been with me through all my years of wilderness-living, gave me a quizzical look but was unimpressed. She, although resigned to them, must surely be puzzled at times by my idiosyncracies.

The immediate drop off to Banana Lake was too steep for me to attempt. I kept along the tree line for a while, but it was very broken and irregular and I soon found myself plunging downwards through a horrible mess of thick spruce, alder, and "misery bush," gravity being my only ally. The dog normally carries her own pack, but she gets hung up and loses it in thick brush, so I had to strap her load on top of mine.

At the bottom of the valley, which was reached after much cursing and swearing, I was on familiar territory: I had now connected with the trap trail I used on my winter trip. But first I had to cross the river — and the crossing was no longer conveniently frozen as it had been before. The bottom looked good, though; it was one of the few places not littered with rocks and foaming with rapids. Close to the bank, the water was knee deep, but it rapidly rose to my waist: too late, I remembered the binoculars in my pants' pocket. I pulled them out but one of the lenses was flooded and ruined.

It was much harder to find the trail without a snow machine track to guide me. In the winter, the trapper had used what was then the easiest way, right up the middle of the swamps of which there were a considerable number. I could get no wetter after my river crossing, but it was very tiring to walk on the tussocky, yielding ground.

It is now the middle of a dull and buggy afternoon and, weary and fly-bitten, I am staring at my crumbling dream. Was it always as rocky as this? The logs for my first cabin were hauled by horses; here I would be totally alone. Even if I had them, horses could not work on this ground. It is so rough that the wheelbarrow I have added to my stock of tools will be useless: I can't even see a place flat enough to pitch a tent.

And yet, while I have been sitting here, my eyes have been sizing and measuring. If I can move that rock, and cut down that tree, and squeeze in between those two boulders, perhaps I can fit a small foundation there. The door could go here; the porch over that hollow: this tree would have to come out, and that one would make a good foundation log.

I can still cancel the project and now is the time to do it, before I become too hopelessly embroiled. One of the criteria that attracted me to this lake was that it is big enough for a float plane to land on — all the freight that came into the Atnarko had to be backpacked two miles, but here everything can be flown to the door. A load of equipment is due in tomorrow; all I have to do is tell the pilot to take it straight back out again and I will not lose a lot, just a bit of time and cash — and a certain amount of face.

But then maybe, just maybe, something can be done with my rocks. I'll sleep on it (if I can find anywhere smooth enough to lie down) and make my decision in the morning.

CHAPTER 2

June 28, 1988

The first day without wind. So far, when the wind has dropped at all, the bugs have become a nuisance, but at the moment it is too cold for them: only 4°C when I shivered through a bath this morning.

It is now afternoon. I sit, muffled in clothes, in my sleeping bag, in the tent, under a tarp, listening to the drumming rain. The tent is an old, canvas one, on its last legs, but it was a good one once and I hope the tarp will extend its life for the summer. It smells of mould and the openings are small and mean — a plus for weather protection, but not a very interesting place to spend long periods of time.

This is the best location that I could find for it, right on the edge of the little swamp just north of the claim. It is not a very smooth site, but the rocks here are cushioned with crowberry and, by bending my body around them when I lie down, I am actually quite comfortable. Another rock, padded with a sweater, makes a convenient pillow. I've guyed the tent to trees and the tarp forms a porch in front and a long lean-to behind. It is back a bit from the lake but, although the stunted, dripping, greeny-grey trees visible through the narrow doorway block the view towards the mountains, they also give me some shelter from the wind. A constantly flapping tent is very wearisome.

My firepit is right at the water's edge. The wind is much fiercer there, but the country did not give me a lot of choice as to where to put it. A fireplace inland would be too dangerous unless I ripped up a large tract of vegetation, and the resulting eyesore would take more than my lifetime to disappear. So a flat rock completely surrounded by water will do duty as my hearth for the time being. More rocks ring the fire, and on them lies part of a cookstove top, complete with two sets of lids which I can lift off so that the pots can sit inside the holes. This helps concentrate the fire, although when the wind is strong, the flames whip like rags and most of their energy is dissipated. My cooking is very basic — boiled or fried — but for something like bread a certain amount of heat control is necessary, so I must plan to bake on a morning when the day is usually calmer.

Bread. The symbol of stability. A fire means nothing; I make one every time I camp (a small, discreet one, I hasten to say) and completely dismantle it when I move on. My present hearth will be washed every year by the rising spring floods and, when I have finished with it, it will not be long before there is very little sign that it ever supported a kitchen.

But bread, leavened bread that is, indicates permanence. It is never made by nomadic peoples. It takes too much time for the yeast and flour to work. So my first round, brown loaf was more than just a tasty meal, it was perhaps a declaration of intent. I guess it means I am here to stay.

I baked it in a lidded cast-iron pot covered by an inverted canner to give some semblance of an oven. Bread is very forgiving; it can stand a lot of varied handling. I rose the dough once only, directly in the cast-iron pot over a bucket of hot water close to the fire while I cooked breakfast. My makeshift oven tends to burn things on the bottom and leave them uncooked on the top, but with the bread in the enclosed cast-iron pot that was not much of a problem for all I had to do was flip the loaf, pot and all, halfway through. The resulting loaf is heavy; it is just as well that I prefer it that way. I eat a lot of bread, and put all sorts of grains and seeds and powdered milk in it, so it is a meal in itself.

I had arranged with Richard, owner of one of the float plane bases at Nimpo Lake, to bring the first batch of equipment on the morning of the 27th of June. He had often flown over the lake and so he knew where it was, but he had never landed on it. All I remember of it from my other two visits was the almost unbroken shoreline of rocks. At the far end, however, was a gravelly beach about thirty yards long. It was the one place I knew for sure where the plane would be able to come in safely and I had told Richard to meet me there. Richard was due at 7:00 AM. I don't have a watch, but I am always up at daylight, which probably occurs at around 5:00 AM this time of year. Rather than rush through breakfast then gallop around the shore of the lake (with no trail, it would take at least an hour) I took my billy, a little tea, and some oatmeal with me and made a tiny fire while I waited on the beach. It was the last of the food I had backpacked in with me: if Richard did not turn up I would start to get hungry.

He was late, but it is never very easy to adhere to clock times in this country. In summer, the float plane bases at Nimpo are busy and, whereas the time in the air is fairly predictable, that needed to load passengers and freight, plus unscheduled delays such as morning fog, are not. This time, the delay was because the bigger plane Richard had hoped to use, the Beaver, was broken down. He could bring only half the load and would return with the rest later in the day. He flew around the lake a couple of times before he landed and told me he could bring the second load into a small inlet much closer to camp, which was welcome news.

It always amazes me that it is possible to fly those little planes with unwieldy things like canoes strapped to their float struts. The canoe had to come in on the first flight so I could ferry my supplies back to camp. The tent came, too — a heavy canvass lump and an awkward bundle of aluminium poles (I had spent the first night in my little backpacking tent) — plus various tools including one of my chain saws.

By the time the overloaded boat reached camp, the wind had risen and the lake was blurred and choppy. Now that I was in the water, I could see an alarming number of rocks just below the surface around my point. It was rapidly becoming difficult to steer between them and already the canoe risked damage if it was tied up. So I jumped into thigh-deep water between the canoe and the shore and held the boat with one hand while I tossed the gear onto the rocks with the other. Empty, the canoe could be towed into safer shallows and left for a short while. Nearby was a bleached log that had been flung up at the top of some high spring flood, and I dragged it into the water and floated it to where it would make a buffer for the canoe. I wedged a second log higher on the rocks and wired the two together with part of a roll of discarded telephone cable salvaged from a dump; now I had both a crude wharf and a place to haul the boat out of the water without taking the skin off it.

I had just finished when Richard came again. I had to paddle way out into the choppy water to get around the islands and rocks that guard my point. This meant going broadside to the waves and the little boat did not like that at all.

As Richard did not have an external load this time, he was able to bring a lot more freight. There was too much for one canoe load. The food was the most urgent — three garbage cans full; one of which was for the dog — and I left what I could not carry propped higgledy piggledy on the bank. The canoe shipped water going around the point and I figured that I was pushing my luck to fetch what remained, so left it to its fate. The bank on which it sat sloped steeply; the worst that could happen was that a large animal would come along and be curious enough to nudge it into the water.

Bears can never be ignored in this kind of country. My most

urgent job was to build what I hoped would be a bear-proof crate in which to store the three garbage cans of food. It was not without a tinge of guilt that I started up the chain saw. Untouched nature has a special beauty that no man can emulate; each rock, each fallen piece of wood inhabits its own perfect space. It is an aesthetic rightness, impossible to reproduce, like the patina of old furniture.

By simply being here I will damage this fragile bubble. Already a little trail is appearing between my tent and the firepit — heather and crowberry are particularly susceptible to the passage of feet. And with one, sharp five-second burst of the chain saw I had an alien, sharp edge and an ugly, raw pile of sawdust. But I feel that, with care, my impact here will be minimal. There will be no bulldozers or fire to mar the land and I shall do nothing without weighing the environmental cost.

There were enough fallen logs lying around for the food crate. I cut them into eight-foot lengths then flopped them end over end to get them to the site immediately behind my firepit. The notching was very basic and the corners reinforced by ten-inch screw nails (trying to imagine what might fool a bear) and I made a lid of poles nailed closely together on a frame. I wired the back end of the lid to the wall of the crate: this rough hinge will serve well enough. When I leave to go out for mail, I'll wire the front end down, too.

This morning, it being calm, I was of two minds as to which to do first; bake bread or fetch the last of my supplies. My stomach won and the bread prevailed, but luckily the calm persisted and the rest of my supplies are now stowed under the tarp lean-to behind the tent. Those two jobs over with, I grabbed the shovel and went to look for a suitable place for an outhouse. It would have to serve both the cabins I proposed to build, be well away from the lake shore — and be in a place where I could dig.

Two big boulders leaned together at the back of the claim. I think they are actually outside my designated area, but with luck it will be a while before I have to worry about boundary disputes.

Between the boulders there was a ready-made hole — if I could excavate it further it might just do. I poked the shovel between the rocks. Clang; another stone. But it was small enough to chivvy out, as was the next and the next, and I was able to dig down another three feet before I hit a solid base. A structure around the hole is not a priority right now. The flies and inclement weather make it a less than idyllic place to contemplate the universe, but as I am not one of those people who read encyclopedias in the bathroom, it will suffice for the present.

There was still a good portion of daylight left after the excavation, but the hills had grown murky and Mt. Monarch and his consorts were all but hidden in rolls of cloud. Rain was imminent. But there was one other job I wanted to do before my camp was complete.

At the last minute, I had thrown a few packets of seeds into my load of supplies. With a greenhouse and something resembling soil, I expect quite an array of vegetables could be produced here. But having nothing but bare gravel or raw swamp, soil will take years to make and a greenhouse is not practical for, when I go out for mail, or if I am away with parties of hikers (if I ever reach that stage), the greenhouse will have to be left to its own devices for a week or more and either the plants would fry or an animal would destroy the structure. I'm not much of a gardener, but figure a few raddishes and lettuces might grow. Anything fresh will be worth its weight in gold up here. Richard brought carrots and onions and potatoes on the plane, but at this time of year it is very difficult to find vegetables that keep well; anything in the local stores has had a long and tedious journey from California before it reaches them, so only the toughest and most tasteless produce can survive the trip.

So because I expect to be away at times during the growing season, a garden patch will have to be able to look after itself. By poking tentatively with the shovel I found a patch in the little meadow north of the point where the bottoms of the sphagnum moss plants were black and partially disintegrated as opposed to red and undigested as seemed to be the case in most places. I cleaned away the turf and built up a little wall of sods on the windward side. The "quarter inch of fine soil" with which I covered the short rows of

spinach and raddishes was cold and wet and with the consistency of papier mâché. I would imagine, too, that the ground is
extremely acid, so I am not expecting too much from my efforts. I
have started some bean sprouts in a jar, but they will not grow if it
stays this cold. I can do nothing to improve their chances short of
putting them in my sleeping bag at night and I don't fancy a leaking
jar as a bedfellow.

The rain is easing intermittently and it has grown a little warmer.
Mosquitoes swarm beyond the tent's screen and I feel some small
satisfaction watching them whine and crawl impotently only inches
from my head. I suppose I should be content merely to have a place
to get away from them, but I can only feel frustrated by the cramped,
mouldy gloom of the tent and the oppressiveness of the weather. I
want to be up and doing.

CHAPTER 3

June 30, 1988

> *Life*
> *Is so much better*
> *When the sun shines.*

I have fallen my first trees. How twisted and short they are compared with the great fir logs I had for the Atnarko cabin. There are
no Douglas fir here, but I have two species of pine, lodgepole and
white-bark. Lodgepole dominates the lower country east of here. It
is a strong, straight tree with a well-known reputation as a building
material. It will grow almost anywhere, even to the tree line, but at
higher elevations the white-bark becomes more common. The white-
bark is an unusual conifer, for its silhouette is more like that of a
deciduous tree, with a wavering trunk and a many-branched crown.
Both green and dead twigs snap easily and it rots fast as a rule; yet
fire-killed specimens become as hard as iron. There are a multitude
still standing despite the fact that the last fire must have gone through
almost a century ago. For the main structure I needed lodgepoles
but would use the green white-bark for the parts of the building in
which strength was not so crucial.

The first tree I cut down was already dead and leaning against its neighbour. The butt was full of carpenter ants but when I sliced off a couple of stove-lengths I reached sound wood. The tree was knotty and branchy, but otherwise fairly straight and will make an excellent foundation log.

Now I had to get it to the site.

A friend of mine raised all the timbers of his post and beam house with a come-along. He had generously leant this tool to me but I had never used one before; it looked a feeble little instrument to move my great big log. I tied a rope around the butt of the tree, hooked one end of the come-along into it, joined the other with a second rope to an anchor, and I was ready to start. Crank, crank, crank went the ratcheted lever. The cable tightened, the ropes stretched, then, with a jerk, the log shifted a whole inch — and buried its nose against the stump.

Logs are not as formidable to move as is at first supposed, for, compared to other objects of the same weight, they have two advantages: they are long and thin so can be pivoted around a central point, and they can be rolled. An indispensable tool for both these operations is a peavey.

To ease the passage of the log over the stump (which was cut off as close to the ground as was possible) a skid was needed. I peeled it first to reduce the friction beween it and the log. Putting it there was a lesson in co-ordination for when I leaned forward to shove the skid under the log, my weight came off the peavey and the log thumped back down on the ground. But I am a tall person and by employing a spare leg I was able to complete the manoeuvre, the first of many contortions that will no doubt be my lot.

But the log was finally on its way. However, progress was infinitely slow. It took probably an hour to shift that log fifty yards. The come-along cable is short and it must be reset, and the anchor rope constantly readjusted, all of which means a lot of traipsing back and forth when working alone. But now the log lies approximately where it will finally rest, although I still have some notching and rock-manoeuvring to do before I am finished with it.

The second tree was a green one and much closer to the building site. I peeled it to help it slide over the ground more easily, but no knotting in the world would hold a rope on that slimy log. It will eventually need a notch near its end to fit around a rock in the place I have chosen for it, so I sliced a bit out of it and this gave me something to snag the rope around. I will leave a collar of bark to hold the rope on all the other logs that I will need to haul.

I live in a part of the world where many people build their own houses. Many are constructed with little idea of what is going to happen inside them. There is no right way to design a house, for each person will have a multitude of his own requirements and compromises. But the rectangle with windows and door in the middle of each wall, or, worse still, the long tunnel with windows at only one end, is not a lot of use for anyone. The people who do most of the building are men; unless they have some experience of running a house, their main concern is the strength and ease of construction. This cannot be ignored, but the inside of the dwelling is of no less importance.

These are examples of the most common faults I have seen: (a) The stove is too far from a window. This means, in a house without electricity, you either freeze by the window or use a lamp all day by the stove. (b) The only place to sit is between the stove and the door so you are subject to a major draught when outside air whistles in to replace that consumed by the stove. The colder it is outside, the hotter the fire will be, and the greater the draught it will create. (c) The table is so located that either you work at it dazzled by the light that comes through the window, or you sit with the window at your back and the work is shadowed by your own body. (d) And how often is the kitchen area poked into the darkest corner? I am not much of a cook and don't intend to spend half my life in the kitchen, but I still need a good window there.

Climate, needless to say, is a major consideration for any building. Up here, it sometimes gets very cold and I can expect a hefty weight of snow in the winter. My roof must either be strong enough to support the snow or steep enough to shed it. But the snow can be utilized, for in a house without a basement, walls banked with snow are invaluable to stop draughts through the floorboards. I once wintered in a cabin whose floor was rough-hewn logs, the gaps between which were up to three inches wide. As soon as there was enough snow to bank the walls, I was never cold. But banking can be effective only if every part of the building can be treated that way. It is of only limited use to bank three walls and leave the fourth open as happens with cabins that have a porch built directly onto extended foundation logs. My porches will have separate foundations made lower than those of the interior of the cabin so that no part of the living area will be left unbanked.

The purpose for which a building is to be used is also a very important consideration in the design. I will live alone, but plan to accommodate as many as ten people here in two cabins. The larger cabin will also double as a part-time studio and living space for myself and I want storage space for art supplies and books as well as food and clothes.

Cost is another major factor to consider. The land and a lot of the building materials will be comparatively cheap, but I will rely heavily on all manner of things from the outside world that will not only cost money in themselves, but will be enormously expensive to transport. The nearest shopping centre is at Williams Lake two hundred miles to the east, and even there prices are a great deal higher than in Vancouver because of the road freight. Not only do I have to truck the stuff to Nimpo Lake on top of that, there is also the airfreight, which will probably amount to about a quarter of my summer's expenditure. Having to fly all my stuff in creates further problems, for everything has to fit into, or be tied onto, a small, single-engined plane.

"But how do you know where to begin?" city friends ask me when I tell them I am going to build a house. The only answer is to start at the bottom and work up. The two logs that I have hauled will form the foundations for the east and west walls of the cabin. (They are not exactly east and west, but it is easier to think of them that way.) They will require a lot of adjusting, for most of the rocks will not budge and the logs will have to be notched to conform. I want the logs clear of the ground to prevent them rotting, but they must also be as low as possible for every inch of height at this level means extra lifting at the top. Also, the lower the building, the less an eyesore it will be.

But the adjusting of the foundation logs will have to wait until tomorrow for the daylight is already going. Two logs does not seem a lot to have accomplished on my first building day, but I am well pleased with myself, for if I can move those, I can shift anything I am likely to need.

July 5, 1988

I am taking advantage of another calm morning to bake bread again. I tried leaving the dough to rise overnight, but it was too cold and so I am sitting here, monitoring it over a low fire. This surely beats the watched kettle into a cocked hat.

I ought to be glad of a chance to slow down a little. Falling trees, peeling them, and hauling them is punishing work. Even when I stop for meals it is difficult to relax; either it is too cold or the bugs drive me crazy. I am probably the most delectable feast to come their way for many a generation. My eyebrows itch. I think the flies must line up on top of my glasses and take aim.

Each tree takes so long to deal with that I seem to be making no progress. Number four, the last of the foundation logs, was a brute to haul — I swear it was grinning at me. On its cut end were two knots like slanted eyes and a peculiar mark like a smirking mouth under the round core of the nose. I fought with it every inch of the way; it took half a day to bring in. I was talking to it by the time I had finished with it, and had perverse satisfaction every time it buried its grinning face in the dirt.

And yet, things are happening on the building site, for not only are the foundation logs down, but four floor joists, flattened roughly on the top, are also notched into place. Several more trees have been pruned from the cabin site, not just from within the foundations, but on the windward side as well. Almost all the trees lean away from the prevailing wind and I cannot leave any that might be a potential danger once the place is built. Unfortunately, few of these are any good for building: their only use will be as firewood. I begrudge the time I have to spend limbing them and bucking them so that I can clear them out of the way. The thought of the massive clean up after the cabin is built makes me wince every time I cut down a tree. It would be far too dangerous to attempt to burn the brush at present and, in any case, I have no desire to emulate the black holocaust created by clear-cut logging that I see every year when I go tree-planting. I'm not quite sure how I'll deal with all the brush yet. Chopped up, it will make excellent summer cookwood, giving a fast, hot fire that will die out quickly and not overheat the cabin. But it will be years before I can burn all the brush in that way. The building season will be short; I can't afford the time to do anything but leave most of the brush wherever it falls at present. The raw stumps are like wounds. I shall cut them all flush with the ground eventually and many will be hidden by the ground cover, but there will be some in the open that will always be visible and an accusation.

One such stump belongs to a tree that was probably the biggest in the area, a good two feet through for the first twenty feet of its length. But at chest height it had developed a massive kink and the great trunk leaned at a very sharp angle, dangerously close to the cabin. So down it had to come. It was almost completely rotted through at the kink, but the rest of the tree looks fine and I will use it to make floorboards.

Another tree caused what at first appeared to be a disaster. It was only a light tree — I thought it might make a good ridge-pole — but I had to fall it so that it landed right across the floor joists, which I had already nailed down. I feared for them, but they did not so much as splinter: it was the south foundation log that broke. It collapsed where a massive notch had been cut out of it, but even then it should have held. However, I remember that it had been a devil to peel, and the break was woolly-looking, both evidence of disease; but I did not realize how much the tree had been weakened by it. My first reaction of rage at having to repeat all that laborious work was followed by one of relief that it had happened now and not when half the building was standing on it.

No matter how carefully I choose a tree, I never know whether it will answer its purpose until I have it on the ground. I thought one unusually straight tree might make a good plate-log (the log that runs along the top of a side wall: the rafters are notched to it), but it proved to have a peculiar rot in the butt. By the time I reached sound wood, the log was barely long enough for a floor joist. The very next tree had a different kind of rot and it became worse further up the stem; the top of the tree had almost disintegrated inside. And yet the living tree had looked perfectly sound and healthy.

A rotten tree can be very dangerous to fall. Providing there are no obvious difficulties like severe lean in the wrong direction or obstacles in the way, the direction of a healthy tree is easy to control by the angle of the cut and the relative thicknesses of both ends of the hinge. But a rotten tree can collapse much sooner than expected and in an unpredictable direction. The resistance of the tree to the saw and the colour of the sawdust are the best indications that all is not perfect, but they are not infallible. The type of weakness that had afflicted the broken foundation log is very difficult to predict.

Another danger is the rocks. If a tree hits one part way along its trunk when it is falling, either the butt can whip around or the whole tree can bounce so I must be prepared to leap well out of the way. I hate falling trees. I hate the saw, its hideous screeching, and its danger. The thought of being crushed is never out of my mind.

The most impressive part of my building is not the foundations, however, but an upright: a corner post. A traditional horizontal-log cabin would be difficult to construct here, for I would be hard put to find enough tall, straight trees. So, partly because of that, and partly because I am a poor, weak, helpless female and will be working alone, I have decided on the piece-on-piece method of building. This comprises uprights approximately eight feet apart, with short horizontal logs slotted in between. I have never seen a piece-on-piece building, but see no reason why I can't make it work. I will still need long timbers for the foundation and the roof, but I think there are just enough tall lodgepoles around for the purpose.

I hauled the eight-foot, newly peeled log onto the floor joists and cut out the grooves that would hold the pointed ends of the fillers. Ripping, in other words, cutting along the grain of wood as opposed to across it, is very hard work for both the chain saw and the operator. Neither of my saws seem to be working well: the new Husqevarna 35 is spluttering and the 266, which has weathered, without serious problem, all the years of use and abuse that I gave it at the Atnarko, seems to be underpowered. So ripping is slow and tedious work and after eight cuts, each eight feet long, my back is not too happy.

It was not until I had finished the grooves that I realized that I was going to be unable to lift the green, heavy post without some assistance: I would need a gin pole. I hunted in the bush and found a slim, dead tree that seemed both tall and strong enough to use and light enough to lift, something that is extremely rare here. I tied the butt of the gin pole to the corner of the foundations and guyed the top to stumps. It had started to drizzle, which made the newly peeled post unbelievably slick. I began to crank. The guy ropes twanged tight, the top of the gin pole bent a little, but the post began to lift off the ground. Too late, I realized that the gin pole was not long enough after all and the come-along had wound itself up when the post still had a couple of feet to go. Could I tip the balance by brute force? I wrapped my body round the sticky post and heaved. The drizzle had turned to rain and my footing on the floor joists was very insecure. I thought I wasn't going to manage it, but I was just able to wriggle it onto its seating — only to find it wouldn't stay there for the gin pole had been pulled forward and was now in the way. The bugs chose this moment to home in. Somehow I was able to slacken and readjust the guy ropes while still hugging the corner post, then ease my burden into place. At once it was lashed to the gin pole with bits of string I had put in my pocket, then braced securely with diagonals attaching it to the foundation logs. I spent a long time squinting past the edge of a spirit level to make sure that the post was as vertical as possible before I banged in the nails of the diagonals. Then I rushed off to fetch my camera to record this momentous occasion. The post stood tall and golden like the column of a ruined Greek temple — perhaps not the best analogy for a building barely begun.

I will need five more short uprights, three of them corner posts and two longer ones for the centres of the east and west walls. Raising them will require a lot more planning and I'm not yet sure how I'm going to do it.

The bread has puffed up at last so now I can boost the fire and bake it, which is a relief as it is rather chilly sitting here with the fire banked low. It is a gloomy day, but there are some very beautiful moments when soft gleams of light poke beneath great piles of cloud, all quiveringly reflected in the lake. The mountains are playing hide and seek; every time I look at them, they are different.

I have a little fox sparrow for company. She scrapes the duff furiously with frantic jerks of her body that put a chicken to shame. She is often here while I am beside the fire. She covers the same piece of ground that she has harvested many times before, but she always seems to find something new.

And now it is starting to rain again. I am like Itsy Bitsy spider, up and down with the weather. Was he, when he climbed the spout a second time, an optimist, or just plain stupid? Was his achievement a fine example of the rewards of persistence, or a study in futility?

CHAPTER 4

July 11, 1988

I leave for the highway tomorrow. I intend to make a start on the trail. The major features on the route such as lakes and rivers are easy to find, but the brushy stretches between them will need a lot of sorting out. I have a couple of rolls of flagging tape with me and I will start ribboning trees from this end of each section until I am obviously off course, then, when I come back, start marking from the other end, hoping that I will meet somewhere. The awkward bends and kinks can gradually be ironed out each time I pass through. When the route is finally established, I will dispense with the ribbons and brush out and blaze the trail properly. One section I want to deal with as soon as possible is the piece that was so steep and dense above the river crossing. I don't want to have to face such a wearying tangle every time I go back and forth.

It has suddenly become miraculously hot. For once, the extra breezy coolness of the firepit is very welcome. The mosquitoes have subsided and the cool, fresh, calm mornings are glorious. Long before they reach me, the rays of the rising sun touch the tip of Mt. Monarch with pink, then swiftly turn to orange, then gold, then yellow, then cream, then blinding white as they flood the wall of eternal snow. (Eternal, at any rate, since the last ice age.)

Temptation finally overcame me this morning and I abandoned my great intentions and slid the canoe into the water. It was high time, in any case, that the dog had a good run. She learned as a puppy to keep well out of the way when I am using a chain saw and she spends the day alone and bored in camp.

While the dog scrambled along the rocky shore, I paddled around the two islands that jut out from the point, marvelling at the new, golden uprights, pencil-thin and alien, that I could now see rising from the tangle of underbrush on the shore. The second island is right at the tip of the point, then comes a much smaller island with a stump on it, and finally a big round island. Its eastern end is opposite the inlet where Richard dropped my freight. Behind the first inlet is a second one and, way at the back of the lake, is a narrow, crescent-shaped island that runs parallel to the shore and is almost cut through in two places.

I drifted dreamily close to the shore. How wonderfully the wind-blasted trees have arranged themselves over the rocks: the rich, yellow-green lodgepoles; the stragglier, slightly bluer white-barks (their needles are in clusters of five, as opposed to the two of the

lodgepoles, and they have a looser, shaggier look); the wide, sweeping skirts of the balsam firs; the prickly, ground-hugging junipers; the tangled broad-leaved mountain alders. The Labrador tea and swamp laurel have all but finished flowering, but a few purple fleabanes are out and the white buds of the fringed grass of parnassus are showing. Each leaf and flower inhabits its allotted space. How impossible it is to try and jam nature's subtle compositions into the boundaries of a rectangle of cellulose.

I had drifted close to Big Island, when there was a loud splash: coming towards me, swimming in the water, was a large bull moose. His antlers were well developed and the fur on them was backlit by the early sun so that they were rimmed with platinum fire. I have often canoed right up to moose for they appear to have no programmed fear of boats. But when this one saw me, he ignored convention and turned round and swam back to the island as fast as he could. There was a splash as he heaved himself out of the water, a great crashing of brush as he barged across the island, and another splash as he jumped into the lake on the other side. I thought that would be the last of him but, some time later when I had forgotten about him, I heard a fainter, distant splash close to the outlet across the lake, followed by still further crashings as the poor animal continued to depart the scene at the maximum possible speed. The sound of the breaking brush eventually faded into silence. How many years had that animal wandered this lake alone? Meeting a human being was obviously the last thing on his mind.

I passed the First Inlet, then the Second, and rounded the back of the lake. I could now look up towards the mountains whose dazzling walls were framed by the groups of trees that sprang up from the water. The bulk of the lake was already aquiver, but the water behind the island was stirred only by the brief passage of the canoe, before becoming motionless and reflecting the mountains in every faithful detail. How quiet! How utterly still!

Crescent Island is almost joined to the shoreline at its southern tip, but I was just able to ease the canoe beween rocks. It was not far from there to the outlet where the lake tumbles into rapids and continues its journey down the valley. Somewhere along here, Moose had made his exit. The song of the river increased as I drew near; the canoe nosed into its opening, but rocks barred the way like teeth. There was a sudden puff of wind. The lake shivered, then jumped instantly into a lively, blue chop. That's the way the wind always seems to start here. Back to camp I went before the waves grew too uncomfortable; in any case, it was high time to start work.

The work appears to progress desperately slowly. But I have to remind myself that I have been here only two weeks and, as with all new experiences, it seems a lot longer, therefore I expect my accomplishments to be greater. However, when I sit back and look at what I've done, I now have a very obvious structure.

Perched on the little bed of rocks are four foundation logs, four floor joists, seven short uprights (the odd number is because of a doorpost — I'd forgotten about that in my original calculations), also four filler logs in place, plus two more fillers and the two fifteen-foot end posts, cut and ready to be raised, lying on the floor joists. They will stay there for a while so that they can dry out a bit. A huge amount of water is lost in the first week or two the tree is down, providing the log is peeled (if it isn't, it hardly loses any) so, rather than doggedly raise each tree as I cut it, I have been falling and peeling all my roof poles, ticking them off, one at a time, from a list scribbled on a bit of paper that I carry in my shirt pocket. There are: three twenty-three footers, two fourteen footers, eighteen rafters, and ten ceiling joists. Most of them have come from the far side of the swamp, some distance from the cabin, as that is where small stands of younger lodgepole grow. A few really good trees stand just behind the outhouse, but I want to save those for the second cabin. It will be bigger and will require the longest logs.

Scattered about the place are a number of fallen trees that are hung up on rocks or their neighbours and that are therefore still sound. They are all weathered to some degree; the white-barks have attained a lovely, soft, silver colour. It will save both living trees and work if I use them but, rather than mix them with the new, yellow logs, I will make a complete wall of them; the east wall behind the stove where the kitchen area will be. In the piece-on-piece method of building, each section of wall can be worked separately. I will leave that part until last for it is from that direction that most of the building components are dragged. The door hole not only faces the wrong way, but overlooks a sharp drop, which makes it awkward to use. The rest of the walls will be worked on as a unit so that all the fat, heavy logs will be on the bottom and the lighter ones on the top.

When I came to fit the first filler, I ran into another problem. The fillers are pointed at the ends and are designed to fit snugly in the grooves that run up the posts. But the distance between the backs of the grooves is greater than that between the flanges. How could I squeeze the filler in? The most obvious way was to lift the filler the complete height of the posts and slot it down. But the thought of the enormous structure I would have to construct to complete this operation was too daunting. So I have cheated and cut the flanges off the inside of the corner posts. The slabs that I have removed will be kept and pinned back to hide the ragged joinery and nails when the building is finished.

No one will ever know.

Scribing, a more professional type of joinery that marries horizontal logs together, is inappropriate for these green and twisty fillers so I will merely run a chain saw between them a time or two to smooth out the worst of the lumps. They will need chinking later, but that can wait until the roof is on.

I have been checking my "garden" periodically. Nothing happened until the warm weather came, now rows of cress and raddishes have popped up with a vengeance. So maybe something will come out of it after all.

I am delighted to discover a very interesting flower that is starting to bloom along the waterfront at the edge of the swamp. It is one that I remember reading about as a child, but that did not grow in the part of England in which I was raised. It stuck in my mind because it was an insect-eater, which conjures up all sorts of horror-movie images, but this is a most benign and pretty plant, having a rich purple flower reminiscent of a violet. It is called the butterwort.

Insect-eating plants occur in bogs where nitrogen is either not present or unavailable due to high acidity. Each species has a different method of catching its prey: the pitcher plant attracts its food with enticing aromas and then lures the insect into its receptacle where it is dissolved and digested; the bladderwort, a free-floating plant that comes closer to the movie image because it is triggered into movement, has little underwater traps which can close on microscopic creatures in 300 milliseconds. The sundews and butterworts rely on sweet-smelling, sticky substances on their leaves to entrap their victims: digestive enzymes then convert the animal into a form that can be assimilated. I once saw a sundew bog completely a-glitter with millions of damselfly wings; there was no trace of the inch-long bodies. The enzymes were made use of in Scandinavia, for butterwort was used as a vegetable rennet to curdle milk. I thought it might be interesting to try this, but when I saw the black specks on the plant's leaves, which presumably were the remains of its dinner, I was not so sure I wanted to experiment.

I wonder if my truck is still where I left it? The fifteen-mile mud wallow that brought me from the highway ends at a ranch and resort, currently unoccupied, on the shores of Charlotte Lake. It has an absentee American landlord and is staffed by caretakers. I used to know the people there, but there are new caretakers now. When I tried to drive to the ranch on my way in, I was halted by a locked gate adorned with such a fearsome barrage of "keep-out" notices that I returned to the forestry campground, which lies a couple of miles before the ranch, and left the truck there.

A few clouds threatened this afternoon, but the piled, gilt-edged remnants are now sailing quietly past the mountains and it is a truly beautiful evening. I never lift my head in this place without being thrilled anew.

CHAPTER 5

July 27, 1988

I am sitting on the south side of the point in the early morning sun. My seat is one of three hefty logs that I have winched down from the bank and coerced into lying on some shallow rocks at the edge of a steep drop into the water. This will, I hope, provide a suitable wharf for the plane that I have booked for this morning (if I've calculated the date correctly). The improvised wharf is directly below what I hope will be the site of my second cabin. I cannot see the mountains at the head of the lake from here, but instead look directly towards the outlet, which, from this angle, is flanked by Stump Island and Big Island. Before I left, I investigated the channel between these two islands and found it to be deep and rock-free, so it should be safe for a plane. Behind the islands rise the hills over which I travelled on the first part of my journey to the road.

Two miles downriver from the outlet is a confluence where a much bigger stream joins my branch of Whitton Creek. This is where I pick up the trapper's trail. It keeps north of the river and follows its general course down the valley, rounding Banana Lake, crosses to the right bank below it, and continues to Charlotte Lake. But the river crossing I wanted to use was halfway between the confluence and Banana Lake, just below a rough little cabin erected by the first person to trap this area, an old native, long since deceased, named Sam Sulin. The cabin was on the south side of the river and not visible from the left bank, but I remembered where it was from my winter trip. I also remembered to take the binoculars out of my pants' pocket when I waded into the water to cross over to it this time.

Most trappers do not need space for libraries or art work, and most of their cabins are only three or four logs high with barely enough room to crawl around in. This one, however, was taller than most. The current trappers, a couple with an eight-year-old boy, had thrown new poles, plastic, and a layer of sods over the crumbling roof and built a door of chain-sawed boards which swung on store-bought hinges. They had furnished it with a long, rusty heater made of two five-gallon cans mated together, and a warped, tin cookstove hung on top. In one corner was a shelf which supported a few things like coffee and soup mix (although few containers held the contents advertised by their labels), plus a stack of enamel plates, a can bristling with cutlery, a bottle with a stub of a candle bleeding all over it, and a little pile of dog-eared, dusty, but eminently readable paperbacks: a Le Carré spy story, *Love Among the Butterflies*, Wilfred Thesiger's *Arabian Sands*, *Mutiny on the Bounty*. Two log rounds and a tapered, wooden packbox served as seats; the bed was the wood-chip floor. The windows were small and glassless, sealed with plastic in the winter and shuttered in the summer with the metal from flattened fuel cans nailed on with three-inch screw nails. The door was fastened with a bit of wire twisted around a nail. Outside there was a hitch-rail for horses, a loose stack of firewood, an old axe with a very loose head, and an empty forty-five-gallon drum on the porch. Hardly the fanciest place, but sheer luxury in inclement weather. By the time I arrived there, it was raining again.

Above the cabin was the thickest part of the brush. Coming down the river, the valley wall had been visible once or twice and I had noted a bare rock slide that fell well below the tree line. If I could reach that, and if it proved reasonably stable, it would save me a lot of bush-bashing.

I had left home early so the day was still young. I put my gear inside the cabin and started up the mountainside, ribboning profusely as I went. The valley wall grew steeper, the bush grew shorter and thicker, but at last the rock slide was before me. It was perhaps half a mile across, but appeared to be quite usable. Well pleased with my afternoon's work, I slithered back down through the dripping brush and spent the night in the cabin.

I had brought the bow saw and a pair of long-handled clippers with me and the following morning I started to hack and chop a way to the rock slide. I could not hope to brush out the whole section in one day and had neither the time nor the food with me to spend more than one extra night on the trail, so after a few hours I strapped the tools to my back, followed the ribbons to the rock slide, and mapped out the next stretch of the journey. I was further to the west and

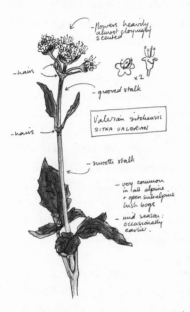

- flowers heavily, almost cloyingly scented
- hairs
× 2
- grooved stalk

Valeriau sitcheusis
SITKA VALERIAN

- hairs
- smooth stalk

- very common in tall alpine & open subalpine lush bogs
- mid season: occasionally earlier.

quite a bit higher than when I hiked in, but although the extra altitude meant more effort, it was well worth it as the views down to Banana Lake were superb. After the rock slide, a narrow avalanche chute, carpeted with crowberry, took me above the tree line. How glorious it was up there. The rain clouds had broken a little and vivid sun and shadow patches chased each other over the mountain. The snow buttercups and globe flowers that were blooming when I first came over had faded away, but the meadows were rife with purple daisies, red paintbrushes, white valerian, and yellow senecios.

I camped on the other side of Maydoe Pass at Top Lake again (not so windy, but wetter this time) and kept much closer to Maydoe Creek on the way down in the hopes of finding a better route than the one by which I had come up. I was largely successful, but ran out of flagging tape long before I reached the road.

The truck was where I had left it, and I began the long, slow drive to the highway. The puddles on the forestry road are large and very deep, but they are not as bad as they look, for the bottoms are solid. Nonetheless, over the years there have been several attempts to find easier routes and the road branches and rejoins many times. Often the alternative is just as worn as the original and it is a toss up as to which branch to take. It is rare to meet another vehicle on the road, but on this occasion I had just started on one of the short detours when another truck lurched onto the far end of it. The road is single lane, so I backed up and drove onto the other branch. At which the other driver promptly did the same. This seemed a bit peculiar because we would now have to find a place where we could both edge off the road to pass each other. However, when we drew abreast and stopped, the driver said to me, "Is that your truck? It was parked so long at the campground, I thought it was stolen and reported it to the police." When I explained my dilemma, the man said that he was the current caretaker and when I returned, I could come to the ranch and leave the truck there. This man was temporary and expected to depart in a few weeks but more permanent caretakers were due before the end of August. I assured him I would contact the police at Anahim and explain what had happened.

I drove the 170 miles to Williams Lake and bought a pile of equipment including more lumber and the sheets of metal roofing that I had ordered when I passed through the town earlier in the year. Williams Lake is in a depression and it suffers badly from the inversion effect: sometimes the smog from the mills is so bad it is hard to breath.[2] Through the brownish air, the heat was suffocating. The galvanized metal, which protected the enamelled sheets of roofing, was blinding and too hot to touch. There was no room in the cab and the dog had to somehow ride on the load. Even a bed of sacks did little to alleviate her distress. The truck did not like it either. There are some long, slow hills climbing out of Williams Lake and in no time the radiator was popping and steaming. I limped to the Fraser River and parked beside it for a couple of hours until the worst of the heat had eased, but the truck was soon boiling again. There are no more than half a dozen gas stations on the whole 270-mile stretch of Highway 20; the first is at Riske Creek. The attendant figured I was having thermostat trouble. He showed me what to do and leant me his tools and I was able to continue at last. I spent the night along the road and the following morning I drove to the float plane base at Nimpo and piled the freight near Richard's wharf.

The heat was a prelude to a storm. I spent three days on the journey home and they were wet, wet, wet. I thought this was supposed to be a dry part of the world. I have sorted out a lot of the Maydoe Creek side of the trail, but at the head of Cowboy Lake there is a massive swamp; try as I might, I cannot find a way round it. There seems no alternative but to wade from one end to the other,

---

[2] This has since been remedied by catalytic burners.

knee-deep in water, a distance of close to half a mile.

Camping was not much fun. It rained and it blew and the fires that cooked my food provided little comfort. I had a dry set of clothes to sleep in, but it was miserable pulling wet clothes on again in the morning. One night, the dog growled then barked furiously. Usually, she is remarkably silent; the only thing that makes her bark is a bear. I had seen droppings and tracks and places where rocks had been overturned, so I knew that there were bears about. As I lay alert and rigid in the clammy, pitch-dark tent, there was the splash, splash, splash of something running away in the water. But it was a moose, I think, by its rhythm.

I looked forward to the comparative comfort of old Sam's cabin, but there I had a shock. For since I had been there, a bear had broken in. It was not so much what it had done to the interior that bothered me, although the place was a mess with everything off the shelves and cans of baking powder and coffee riddled with holes as if they had been peppered with a shotgun, it was the damage he had caused to get in the building that was so appalling. He had ripped up the doorsill, a four-inch-thick chunk of wood nailed down with ten-inch spikes, and clawed off most of the surroundings of the door-frame. Incredibly, the thin thread of wire had held the door. So he had turned his attention to the shuttered windows, ripping off the nailed, tin covering as if it was tissue paper, and climbed in that way. Generous tufts of slightly crinkly black bear hair were snagged onto the remaining nails around the frame.

The trappers will not come this way until the fall when they will horse-pack their trapping supplies to their caches around the line. I don't know if our paths will cross, but I will leave a note for them in their mailbox next time I am out at Nimpo.

I was not a little alarmed to find that a bear had been around my camp, too. At first I was not sure — the pots and pans that I had left upturned against a log were scattered somewhat, but almost anything could have done that. But then I saw that a garbage can lid had been worked off under the lid of the food crate. I could imagine the bear standing on the crate and reaching a paw between the thin poles of the lid, levering away with his claw. Fortunately, nothing inside the can had been touched — he obviously had not tried very hard. Then I smelt the gas. My fuel cans are stored several yards away from both the food crate and the fire. There are, or were, three of them: the centre one was lying on its side, completely empty. In the top were five tiny holes, a bear-claw's distance apart. The bear must have reached into the stack of cans and playfully pulled it out. I was very lucky. It did not seem to be the same bear that had devastated Sam's cabin, for I imagined the camp would have had a very different aspect.

So the first thing I did when I returned home was reinforce the lid of the food crate, and the second was to build this wharf. The sun is climbing higher; no longer does its reflection hang below it, a second sun, in the lake. It now shines full into the water below the wharf. I have dragged away a lot of branches from a fallen tree that might have been a problem for a plane, but there are still a few I have been unable to reach on the bottom. They and the cascade of rocks are covered with a fur of growth which is absent from the shallow, wave-washed gravel on the camp side of the point. It is much more sheltered from the wind here. Finger-sized fish scull close to the surface of the water, investigating the shadow thrown by the new wharf logs. The fish are so much creatures of light themselves they are hardly visible but their synchronized shadows dart and wheel over the bottom; occasionally, one mouths the surface and quivering rings of light radiate briefly over the yellow silt below.

I hear a plane, but there have already been half a dozen this morning. Some go to a lake in a high valley about ten miles behind Big Island. Despite its altitude — for it is higher than this one — it is a popular lake for fishing. Other planes fly steadily towards the west taking tourists to see the glaciers.

But this has to be Richard. He has swooped low over Crescent Island, and is shooting up the lake in a V of spray. I can see lumber strapped to the float struts; he is turning and taxiing in between the islands, and heading straight for my wharf.

August 1, 1988

Richard was not greatly enamoured of my wharf. The plane's float was well cushioned by the outer log, but the tip of its wing fouled trees along the shore. "Just whack them off, and then your wharf will be fine," said Richard, cheerfully. But I want those trees. The main culprit is a great dead lodgepole, long denuded of bark, whose silvery grey limbs sport wiry chartreuse tufts of a plant known as "wolf moss." I love this snag. It is elegant and unusual. Richard exploded with laughter. "This country's full of dead trees," he said. "What on earth do you want to keep this one for?" But the snag excites the artist in me. We live in what must be the only society in the world to separate art from life and condemn it as an unnecessary frill or, even worse, a hobby. And yet everyone is an artist whether they know it or not. Who does not have preferences regarding the type of clothes they wear or the car they buy? These are inescapably aesthetic, or artistic, decisions. Advertising would be useless if people did not have an aesthetic core on which it could act — in the USSR this was very well understood, which was why it was banned.

I am not suggesting everyone should revere a Pissarro or drool over the Mona Lisa. There was a time when I would have been baffled by such things and there is a great deal in the art world that I still don't understand. But much of that is a matter of education, principally an acceptance that such things have a validity. If Richard had said that my tree was ugly, it would have been an aesthetic response and more acceptable as far as I was concerned. But to him it was nothing; just a nuisance to his plane, at best a lump of firewood.

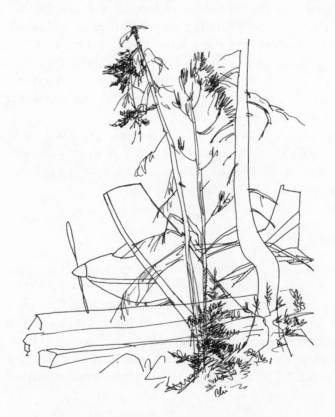

My two end posts are up. Raising them proved time-consuming, but suprisingly easy. My Atnarko neighbours had taught me that almost anything could be shifted with very minimal equipment. Whoever would have thought that those Girl Guide knots and high school lever and pulley lessons would be put to such dramatic use.

For the operation, I needed a longer gin pole and I also needed a ladder. The ladder is only about nine feet long but the rough, wiggly side poles are still heavy enough to make it very awkward to lug about. It is not the actual building of the cabin that takes the time, it is all the fringe jobs. The ladder used most of a precious day, as did the framework to support the gin pole. But once that was up, it all went like clockwork and the raising of the end post took only a minute. The second end post went up just as easily; again, it was the dismantling of the first scaffold and its re-erection at the other end of the building that took so much time.

How tall the structure suddenly seems: it is now possible to visualize the slope of the roof.

One disadvantage of my chosen building method is the number of temporary braces I must use. Diagonals run in all directions and provide added obstacles for me to work around.

When I first came here, I was impressed by the series of crusty, yellow pollen rings on the rocks in some parts of the lake. I was not sure then if the water was still rising or had passed its peak, but now I see that it is falling fast. It is no longer possible to ease the canoe through the rocks close to my camp, so I have dragged it up beside the new wharf.

August 9, 1988

Calm again at last, and for once, quite warm. The last week we have had nothing but gloom and gales. There is still quite a bit of cloud; it shadows the mountains and they preside over their silver-shot reflections in the dark, quiet lake. The windless silence all day was so unusual I kept stopping to listen to it. It was sacrilege to ravage it with the scream of the chain saw; even the clatter of a dish made me wince. I can hear the faint flutter of the fire, the investigative tapping of a hairy woodpecker, the plop of a fish, the whine of a stray mosquito.

It has been a dreary week. Precipitation has not been high and I've been able to work through it, but the incessant wind beats both body and mind. My clothes are perpetually damp and I am always cold. The wind thrums against the tall end posts of the cabin and vibrates them like tuning forks.

And yet, how beautiful it always is. If the sun is shining, the lake is an unbelievable dark, white-whipped blue, beyond which the mountains shine with the purity of alabaster. Today the wind has changed. The clouds are coming from the north, soft stately galleons sailing above their mirror images, striped with silver catspaws.

My "garden" is, not suprisingly, a dismal failure. The little seedlings, which looked so promising when they first came through, never grew taller than half an inch and they have turned yellow and died. I expect that the acidity of the swamp is the problem: I will try lime and fertilizer next year. I am reluctant to attempt to make compost; rotting carrot and potato trimmings could well be too attractive to bears. I have seen no sign of my curious visitor since I have been back and the dog has been relaxed and indifferent, which indicates more than anything else that there are no bears around, but I do everything in my power to avoid encouraging them. This means burning all food scraps and the fish and meat cans the moment they are emptied. Until I came here, I never ate out of commercial cans, but now I live off corned beef and sardines and have to eat a lot of them due to the paucity of vegetables. My meagre ration of sprouts gives me a fresh nibble, but alfalfa sprouts are blah and bean sprouts often rot as it is too cold for them to grow.

When Richard came at the beginning of the month, I arranged with him to return in a couple of days with the roofing — and the vegetables that had been forgotten in his office. But that was nearly ten days ago and there has been no sign of him. I have no means of contacting him short of hiking out. The metal roofing will be an awkward load and perhaps it has been too windy for him to fly with it. In the meantime, the already wilted vegetables must be disintegrating in his nice warm office. I could not leave them outside with the rest of the freight as the risk of both dogs and bears is too great. I have been used to garden-fresh produce most of my life and I sorely miss it.

The cabin progresses. Several of the wall sections have been raised as far as the window sills. The filler logs have every kind of lump and twist. The lowest rounds could be levered into place with the peavey, but I soon found I needed to devise a means of lifting the higher ones. A rope thrown over a ceiling joist tied temporarily to the tops of the posts worked well enough.

It is always a problem to find a straight bit of wood. The young lodgepoles in the swamp must be husbanded carefully as I will be hard pressed to find enough good ones for both cabins. Young white-barks are both too weak and kinked for any building purpose — but they are very pretty. They are delicate and graceful trees with soft bobbles of needles at the end of each slim branch. There is one so close to the north wall of my tent, that for a short time, at sunset, its shadow is projected against the canvas. It makes a classic Japanese brush drawing; the more distant leaves and branches are pale and blurred, the closer ones darker and more sharply defined. This ephemeral work of art will soon disappear forever. The sun sets further round every day and it will soon cease to light the tree. And I most ferverently hope that, by the time the sun gets round this far next year, tent living will be a thing of the past.

One thing fascinates me: the bark of a newly fallen tree is full of tiny mounds of new sawdust, which in a day or two, collect in noticeable piles on the ground. It is probably a type of bark beetle, one species of which is notorious in this area. I believe it is not the beetle itself that kills the tree, but a virus that hitches a ride on the insect. (The man who was supposedly in charge of the beetle eradication programs at the forestry headquarters in Alexis Creek could not elucidate.)

At the turn of the century, the Chilcotin was subject to several very dry years. Man, the manipulator, gleefully set fire to the country, reasoning that if he removed the trees, grass would grow and cattle could be run. At that time the idea that these poor scrubby trees would ever be marketable was so remote that it never crossed anyone's mind; now that everything else has been logged, the industry is fighting over the area.

Grass cannot grow roots long enough to cope with the (usually) scant rainfall in this area. The first thing to come back after a fire is pine. Which means that huge areas of the Chilcotin are all pines and much the same age.

For some intriguing reason, the bark beetle disease attacks only mature trees and that meant there was a colossal outbreak of beetle-kill a few years ago.

People panicked. It was as if the eleventh plague of Egypt had visited them. They talked about the beetle as if it was a sudden, new, malevolent epidemic sprung out of the blue. Their first reaction was to spray it out of existence, but chemicals proved ineffective for by the time the first yellowing needles are noticed, the tree is already dead and the beetle has moved on. Some attempts at control have been made with pheromone traps.

Infected plants die very quickly. Huge patches of dead, standing trees have appeared, in some places both unsightly and a colossal fire hazard. I have several clumps of trees like this around me, but it is not a blanket kill. White-bark pine seem to be just as much affected as lodgepole. Many carcasses are still standing and so are well cured. Those that are not too twisted will make excellent lumber and I will eventually use some of the rest for firewood.

Logging companies have used the beetle as an excuse to clear-cut areas in addition to the annual allowable cut in order not to "waste" the dying trees. But often the beetle-kill proportion of their harvest is pitiably small. And in any case these dead trees have their own purpose, for they provide homes for many animals that are essential for the health of a living forest.

But I don't think that the little piles of sawdust on my newly fallen trees belong to the same bark beetle. At first I thought that they were caused by the insect abandoning a sinking ship but, because the piles of sawdust increase if the tree is not moved, I think they must belong to an insect burrowing in. In which case it must be programmed to attack a tree as soon as it is down. How does the insect know that the tree is no longer living? Does it respond to the sound of the plant crashing to the ground? I know that some woodpeckers do, for at the Atnarko, they would come screeching into the clearing the moment the dust settled after I had fallen one of the big firs. Or is the stimulus some mysterious signal emitted by the plant itself? It could be something undetectable to man, but it seems to me, although this might be my imagination, that the tree smells differently once it has been down for a few hours. Perhaps the chemical changes at the demise of a tree trigger the reactions of the insects.

Certainly something happens to the tree, for unless it is peeled right away, the bark starts to stick. Many of the trees I felled when I first came did not have a designated purpose at the time, but are now being carved up for fillers; some of them are proving very hard to strip.

I hear a plane. It is late for someone to be flying, for behind the clouds, behind the mountains, the sun is going down. It sounds like a Beaver. I do believe it is coming in. It must be Richard!

It was. He didn't like my roofing. The building supply store had had it shipped to Williams Lake in a solid, metal-bound package which weighed four hundred pounds. They'd put it in my pickup with a fork-lift. I and one of Richard's pilots had managed to slide it from there to a pile of lumber at the float plane base. I asked Richard then if he wanted me to crate it differently, but he said no, he could manage. He had braced the package with a few long boards and manoeuvred it (I did not think it politic to ask him how) onto the spreader bars that hold the floats apart. The roofing had dug into the wash from the floats' wake as he'd tried to take off and he thought he'd lost it — he did not know that it was still there until he climbed onto my wharf and could see that it was still in place.

Unloading it was no problem for we cut the metal bands that held the package and slid each sheet off one at a time. This is the roofing for the first cabin only; I will arrange things more conveniently for the second one.

Richard had been delayed all this time because the Beaver had broken down again and the metal would have been too difficult to bring in on the smaller plane. Richard and his pilots can do regular maintenance on their planes, but a licenced mechanic is needed for certain types of repairs and there had not been one available. The Beaver can carry difficult loads and it needs only minimal space for landings and take-offs. But it is incredibly expensive. The floats alone, Richard tells me, cost $60,000, as opposed to a "mere" $15,000 for those of a Cessna 180 or a 185. The floats have a multitude of compartments, each with a different shape that has to be fashioned and riveted by hand.

Well, I have the roofing now — and the vegetables. They are a little worse for wear, but there will be a feast tomorrow. It is growing dark; I am having trouble seeing this page. The mosquitoes are out in force, taking advantage of this warm, calm evening. They have not had much flying weather lately, either.

August 13, 1988

Chilly, but calm again this morning after another two-day blow. A few bits of cloud still pink from the dawn are shredding and flying swiftly from the southwest, so I don't expect it will stay calm for long.

I keep thinking that I'll soon be able to dispense with the come-along to haul building logs, for most of the smaller ones can be dragged, jerk by jerk, with a rope alone. But I keep running into ones that defeat me. I have one more section of wall to complete before I can start on the windows. There are eight sections altogether; one contains the door hole so is in effect only a half section, five will have windows, so only two have to be completed as far as the ceiling, one of these being the back section that I am leaving until last.

I should take advantage of this lull in the wind to fall a beetle-killed tree I have in mind to make the framing for the window holes.

Nonbuilders are often suprised to hear that a log house requires boards, but they need an amazing number unless you are going to use an enormous amount of trees split in half. For the Atnarko cabin I cut every single board — about seven hundred in all, averaging a foot in width and thirteen feet in length. I used an Alaska Mill, a guide bolted onto the bar of my chain saw.

The saw, given its due, was not really big enough for the job. It was slow, excessively noisy, frustrating, tedious work, the most demoralizing occupation I have ever tackled. I am never going to go through that excruciating torture again. In any case, I doubt there would be enough suitable trees here to make all my lumber — notwithstanding the appalling mess that lumber-making makes.

But neither can I afford to buy and fly in all my lumber; so I will have to compromise. The lighter stuff for ceilings and lining the attics I will purchase, and all the heavy two-by-fours, floorboards, and structural elements, I will make myself. The thought of starting the job makes me cringe, but one tree will probably be enough for the window framing.

I have a mystery. Right by my cook-fire, in what was a puddle of water when I first came here, is a pile of freshly picked greens — willow, burnet, roseroot, and purple daisy. Between breakfast and lunch, all the leafy parts disappear and only the stalks are left. Close by, a small hole leads under a tussock of vegetation. Pikas are animals renowned for their hay-making activities, but they live in open rock slides and besides, this hole is too small. It would fit a mouse or a vole, but none of my books indicate that either of these animals collects green plants. In the meantime, these intriguing little piles are there every morning, and they have completely been disposed of by noon.

In Williams Lake, I indulged myself in a new book, *Mosses, Lichens and Ferns of Northwest North America* by Vitt, Marsh, and Bovey. In it is a very interesting story about how "wolf moss," the acid green lichen that grows all over the snag by the wharf, got its name. It was reputedly used, mixed with fat and nails, as wolf bait. Now I find this a little hard to swallow, perhaps even harder than the wolf. My dog does not like carrots. No matter how drowned in gravy the carrots might be, when she has finished her meal, the dish is licked spotless — and so are the pieces of carrots lying in the bottom. If she can so easily separate carrots, I can't imagine that a wolf would have any trouble in picking out nails. However, the book does say that the lichen itself contains vulpinic acid which is a poison in its own right, so perhaps that worked.

I became aware of this lichen not long after I first arrived in Canada, for it makes an excellent wool dye. Alone, it makes a colour very similar to that of its plant (which is by no means normal with most natural dyes), but mixed with things like alder bark steeped with rusty nails, it gives a variety of sea greens, which, however, turn brown if they are washed in alkali detergent! A fascinating study in chemistry.

CHAPTER 6

August 14, 1988

My dog has disappeared. This is very odd as she is usually predictable and faithful and has never been tied in her life. She doesn't wander away from camp, nor does she chase wildlife. In fact, she's so quiet and obedient I forget she is there and I have been neglecting her. I feel guilty when I don't take her for a walk, but I'm too tired to go far at night; it has been too windy to do much canoeing.

When she was not around at lunch time, I was quite puzzled, but now that it is supper time and I have walked around the area and called and called but she still has not turned up, I know that something is seriously wrong.

There is only one thing that I can think of that might have caused her to run off. She is one of those dogs who thinks all human sounds are directed at her alone. At the Atnarko I had owned a cat who was a real brat and always in trouble. But if I yelled at the cat, it was the dog, Lonesome, who hung her head in contrition. Although the camp is some little distance from the building site, Lonesome would have no trouble hearing me — and when things go wrong, which is not infrequently, I have no compunction about voicing my opinion in the strongest possible terms.

Horseflies have taken over from mosquitoes as the major pest and these large, buzzing insects can deliver a very sharp nip. Today, I was standing on a wobbly stump balanced on a floor joist, reaching above my head with the chain saw to smooth the gap between the last two fillers on the north wall. I was tired and hot, glare and flying sawdust were irritating my eyes, and simply having to use a chain saw puts me in a bad humour. So when a horsefly bit me on the throat and I jumped and knocked the insecure stump off its precarious perch, I told the horsefly to "Get the _ out of here," more because of the fright I had than anything else. And the dog, the poor dog, must have taken it personally.

Where will she have gone? She is a real wimp and frightened of most things. She has never run off in the bush, but if she became separated from me outside (for instance if I went into someone else's house), she would always go to the truck. But this time the truck is twenty miles away across a mountain pass. And it is at a place that, by now, will have new occupants — not that they would worry her for she loves all people unreservedly — but if they have a noisy dog she will be frightened of it and won't go to them. She might find her way to Nimpo Lake. I have friends there who own a resort, with whom I always stay when I go out for mail. But they have a big, barky, Newfie cross who terrifies her when she first arrives, although they generally play together after a while.

She might, of course, be somewhere in the bush, trapped or hurt, but if she gets hung up when she is packing, she never makes a sound and I have the devil's own job to find her. I do not have the first idea where to look for her in this case.

There is another aspect to her disappearance. If she does go as far as Nimpo and is recognized, and I am obviously not with her, people might become alarmed about my safety. I always leave my estimated arrival date with my friends at Nimpo as a safety backup, but although they know I am not due out for another twelve days, they also know what a one-person dog Lonesome is. The last thing I want to do is to initiate an unnecessary rescue attempt. So I have no alternative but to go to Nimpo myself. Even if I don't find her I can alert people so they won't be worried if she turns up at some future date.

The tools have been stashed under the tarp lean-to behind the tent, the lid of the food crate has been wired down, and I have written a note explaining the situation and pinned it to the tent's zipper in case the dog has arrived somewhere and someone flies in to check on me. If Lonesome hasn't turned up by morning, which seems unlikely at this stage, I shall have to leave for Nimpo first thing.

August 15, 1988

No dog, so I am going out. Rained lightly and steadily all night so I can expect a wet trip.

August 20, 1988. Noon.

I arrived back at camp about an hour ago — and do I have a tale to tell.

The trip out was wet, enormously wet. It poured and poured with a ferocity that I have rarely seen and certainly would not have expected away from the coast. The same storm, as it moved east, gave Williams Lake more rain than it has had in the last two years put together, and later flooded Calgary to the car tops.

Any dog tracks I might have seen were long since washed away. I was lucky enough to clear the pass before the cloud socked down for good. How thick and dark it was up there — and how the flower meadows glowed in the gloom. They have hung on much later than they normally would; at least something is benefiting from the abnormally wet season.

I was prepared for a night out but, thanks to my marked trail, I was able to reach Charlotte Lake in one day. I stopped only once on the way, when I coaxed a small fire to life to make some tea. I often have a tea break at that particular spot; it is at the top end of one of the small lakes along Maydoe Creek, which I now always think of as Tea Lake.

The truck, when I reached it in the pounding gloom of evening, looked peculiarly red, for I rarely see it free of dust or mud. There was no sign of the dog so I drove to the resort part of the property about a mile away, for that is where the caretakers were living. A sprightly, sixty-year-old woman was in charge, but she was only filling in for her daughter who was to come later in the month. She had with her a fifteen-year-old boy, her grandson, who would be staying on. Another child, his sister, would be arriving with their mother. No one had seen any sign of a stray dog.

So I wallowed through the monstrous puddles out to Nimpo

and asked at the store, the restaurant, and the resorts if anyone had talked about a grizzled, shaggy, very friendly dog; but without success. Then I went to the float plane base to pay for the last flight and told Richard my tale of woe. "Now wait a minute," he said. "I heard someone talking about a dog on the radiophone. I can't remember if they had lost it or found it. It was Buddy Jones. I'll call him and ask him about it."

"Yes, I had a dog turn up here yesterday," came the metallic reply over the radio. "I call it Brew because it is just like the dog on those beer ads." Having not seen the ads in question I could not confirm the description, but it sounded as though it might be Lonesome. But where was Buddy Jones? Richard showed me on the map — and then it clicked. Buddy Jones had a small fishing camp on the mouth of Whitton Creek at the top end of Charlotte Lake. I had passed it on my winter trip, but it had been shuttered and empty then. My dog hates swimming the river so she must have followed the winter trail all the way along Whitton Creek. Buddy Jones would be the first human sign of life that she would encounter and she would be so ready for company then, she would have gone straight over to him.

So back I drove to the dude ranch. Buddy Jones's resort was twelve miles from Rimarko and there was no road to it. If I walked there and back it would take all day. So I asked the boy if he would take me up in the ranch boat. Despite the rain, or more likely because of it, the day was windless, otherwise we would not have attempted it; the lake has a formidable reputation for small boats. We rounded the point and there was the resort, with two planes parked at the wharf. Buddy Jones and a friend, well-slickered, were about to go out fishing. At the sound of my voice, Lonesome immediately ran to me and jumped into the ranch boat. She looked horribly guilty and hung her head. Buddy was a cheery individual who seemed to have rather enjoyed the situation.

Cornwall, the boy from the ranch, was a talkative soul. On the way back, he chatted about his mother and sister and a person called "Alex" who was apparently the fourth member of the family. Alex was tall. Alex drove a truck. "Who's Alex?" I asked. "My mother's lover," said Cornwall, looking me straight in the eye. I thought this a rather out of date term for modern youth to use, but perhaps it is coming into fashion again.

The weather forecast was dismal. The thought of such a dreary trip home was not enticing and, as I would have had to go to Williams Lake again at some time during the summer, I thought I might as well cut my losses and go in the rain.

So I used up another three or four days and it was not until yesterday that I left Rimarko and started back in. The weather was somewhat improved, but it was still unsettled and drizzly. I did some trail work east of the pass, then headed for Sam's cabin, planning to spend the night there and do a bit more on the hillside behind it before continuing to camp.

I had left a note about the bear break-in at the post office for my trapping neighbours when I was out and I had tidied up the cabin a little. There did not seem to be any fresh bear sign. I left the door open when I went to bed so that I would know when daylight came, for with only one tiny window giving light, it was otherwise very dark inside.

I was woken by a furious barking and a hideous snarl. Then silence. Faithful Lonesome, true to form, had barked and driven off a bear. It was barely light. I lay warmly in my sleeping bag and imagined the visitor's round, black rump bouncing off into the bushes. I heard footsteps on the woodchips outside the window that the bear had torn apart. "Good girl, Lonesome," I called sleepily. "Good girl!" There was a massive snort, and a great big bear's nose was thrust into the window hole.

I was electrified. I couldn't find my glasses or the zipper on my sleeping bag, or my boots. All I could think about was the open door and the memory of what the bear had done to it before. Somehow, I found myself standing in the doorway, in my socks. A few yards away was a big, bad-tempered black bear boar.

That black bears are less dangerous than grizzlies is a fallacy. Just read Stephen Herero's *Bear Attacks*. Black bears have been known to stalk and hunt people for food, especially where human beings are scarce and the bears have not learned to fear them.

"Yell," I thought. "Bears don't like noise." "Don't yell," I thought. "Nor does the dog." To hand was the loose-headed axe and the empty fuel drum. I whanged the axe against the drum. The bear charged, ears back, snarling. Backed off. Turned round and started to move away. Swung back and charged again. I simply did not know what to do so stood there banging the axe against the drum. It never occurred to me that the drum had certainly once

contained gas and a spark could have sent both of us to kingdom come. At length the bear turned and ran away.

"Lonesome, Lonesome!" I called. Only the drip of drizzle.

It was still not light enough to see properly. Had the bear killed the dog? Was she lying injured and mute among the trees? There was no way I was going to look for her in a half-dark forest with an angry bear around. I wanted out of there. I thrust everything into the packsack and, clutching my own axe and walking with my head practically screwed round backwards, I waded the river and started to plod up the series of swamps towards camp. I called for a while, but there was no sign of the dog.

It was about three hours after leaving Sam's cabin before I eventually launched the canoe into my lake for the last leg of the journey. And at that moment, a small, white plane circled round, landed and taxied towards me. It was Buddy Jones. He stepped out onto the float, and said, grinning, "I've brought your dog back."

My jaw dropped. Judging by the amount of daylight and the rain, the bear attack must have occurred around 5:00 AM. Buddy Jones was lighting his breakfast fire at 7:10 AM, when he saw the dog outside. The distance between Sam's cabin and Buddy Jones's resort is twenty miles. Lonesome had run it in two hours. And flown back with Buddy in seven minutes.

The dog was ecstatic when she saw me and whined in a way that I have never heard her do before. She must have thought in her doggy way that the end had come for me. She sleeps now beside me as I write, twitching and making little dream yelps in the dappled sunshine.

All's well that ends well, but what a waste of time. I will spend the rest of the day sharpening saws and hauling the boards that I made in the swamp. Tomorrow I will start framing and fitting windows.

CHAPTER 7

August 21, 1988

I seem doomed not to have a smooth run of progress. Something else happened today, and its effects will not wear off so quickly as those of the bear adventure.

I started work on framing the windows. The holes had to fit the miscellaneous collection of glassed and partially glassed frames that I have picked up over the years from dumps and derelict houses. They have been flown in whenever there was space and stacked close to the new wharf. All are small; some of them are single-paned, but many have several divisions. It has been something of a jigsaw puzzle to arrange them so that they will shed light where they are supposed to and yet still keep some continuity in the design of the building.

I carried them carefully, two by two, to the building site, very conscious that if I broke one it would be a long wait before I could replace the glass.

So when I slipped on a sawdust-covered rock while stepping over a floor joist at the cabin, my immediate thought was for the window that I held in my hands; I strived to keep it clear of all the obstacles as I fell. The next instant there was a sickening smack on the side of my head, then a tinkle of breaking glass. My eyebrow had hit the end of a log that lay on the floor joists. I told myself not to panic: head wounds bleed a lot, don't they? Before I moved, I hunted for my glasses which had been knocked into the sawdust. I am near-sighted and the glasses had thin, wire frames; if sawdust was kicked over them, I should never find them again. They seemed fine when I picked them up but I did not put them on right away and later, when I was ready to go back to work, I realized that one lens was completely missing. That was the breaking glass that I had heard: I had saved the window.

I lead a charmed life. I have never hurt myself seriously, in fact this injury was as bad as any I can remember. Fortunately it looked worse than it was, but it is not very comfortable — it is suprising how mobile eyebrows are, particularly when squinting to keep both sun and dust out of the eyes. I expect that if I had been handy to a hospital I would have had a stitch or two put in, but the scar will be in the eyebrow and not very noticeable. I always heal quickly.

It was also suprising how much the lenses of the glasses had previously protected my eyes from flying sawdust. The last time I had an accident with my glasses was when I lost a pair overboard on a cargo boat heading from Singapore to Australia. I have carried a spare pair with me since, a period of some twenty plus years. I have never needed them in all that time, but, inevitably, in this last shuffle of possessions, they have been mislaid. I worked with the broken pair on at first, but it seemed very hard to focus. I realized after a while that the artificial lens distorted things very slightly so that each eye was trying to cope with a different set of signals and my depth perception was destroyed. Fortunately, I am not helpless without them so in the end I put them aside. But I am used to them and I don't like the world to be blurry.

Needless to say, the injury knocked my energy level to zero and I didn't get half the work done that I had expected. Another waste of time. Particularly as it has been a glorious day for once, hot but with a fresh breeze. The sky is cloudless and diamond-clear. The swing of the wind must have brought a change in the weather. I don't know if I dare say it, but it looks as though it is going to last.

August 22, 1988

I have had a bear in camp in broad daylight and I am in a blue panic about it. I heard the dog bark while I was working on the cabin and I hurried to the camp. Lonesome was standing behind the tent, barking lustily and staring excitedly towards the swamp. A stiff breeze was blowing off the lake and away from her so the bear smell can't have been very strong, for she was not too worried. I stared in the direction in which her nose was pointing. Was that a movement behind a clump of balsam about thirty yards away? A gingerish something that wove back and forth? The breeze was lively enough to jiggle the branches and send confusing patterns of light and shadow over everything. And, because of my broken glasses, everything was blurry. Was that a faint growl above the merry singing of the wind and cheerful slap of water against the rocky shore? Squinting hard, I looked and looked. The fuzzy leaves danced and the amorphous shadows flickered. The dog was calming down. Surely there was nothing there now. "Good girl," I said to the dog, making much of her, and she looked pleased with herself.

If this is the bear I encountered at Sam's cabin, I could be in very serious trouble. If he is attracted to my food, his most likely route will be from the swamp to the firepit — which is right past the tent. My camp is poorly designed, but there was simply no alternative.

I wish Lonesome was a little braver. She's fine if a more aggressive dog is with her, for she and her litter mate (who belongs to friends) have treed many a bear between them.

I own a shotgun — but it lies in Richard's office. It had to be kept locked and out of sight so was easily forgotten on his last trip; mine is by no means the only freight that is piled at the float plane base and I don't always label everything as well as I should to avoid confusion. In any case, I am not at all familiar with firearms and have absolutely no confidence that my possession of one will mean instant salvation. I am far more likely to create more problems with it than solve them. I do have a squirt can of capsicum pepper, especially designed as a bear repellant. The pepper severely irritates the eyes and nose of a recipient and incapacitates him instantly. But it works only at very close quarters and, if the wind is wrong, the operator gets it too. I have the dog to consider as well. I can't very well tell her to close her eyes and hold her nose and run for it.

The only other weapon I have is a chain saw. Those unprotected ripping teeth give me the horrors. Its noise might be enough to deter a bear and the whirling chain will give me something to fight back with in the event of an attack. It is the big saw that I will have to pack around with me. The little one would be easier to carry, but it takes a lot of pulling to start; the big one is far more reliable.

I am sitting beside the fire, trying to eat supper. It tastes of cardboard. I jump every time the dog raises her head and turns it towards the swamp. It looks as though it will be a clear night so I think I'll pack my foamy and sleeping bag onto the wharf logs and spend the night there. I will then be well away from any bear that wants to investigate my camp. I will take the capsicum squirt can and the saw and keep the canoe in the water ready for a quick getaway. How I wish my cabin walls were solid enough to give me protection. I hope the bugs won't be too bad without a tent.

August 23, 1988

A panic over nothing I think. An uneventful and somewhat uncomfortable night, but a very beautiful one. The growing moon's track is very low at this time of year and it set early, but the stars were so large and soft that the night never seemed to get really dark. Occasionally a fleeting streak of light presaged the passage to oblivion of some microscopic cosmic particle. The water, rarely still, made tiny lapping sounds beneath the wharf. The sun rises behind Big Island now and the cloudless dawn put clear green, then lemon, then a rich, burnt orange behind the multi-branched silhouettes of the white-barks on the island. It all had a strangely tropical look, as if screeching monkeys with swinging tails were about to leap in racing bands against the Salvador Dali sky.

August 26, 1988

At last I am getting somewhere. The framing for the windows is finished, and the remaining pieces of wall that surround them are completed. Because of the open back section, the structure now looks like a film set, three-sided and false. According to the tape measure it is pretty well square, but the twisted nature of some of the components gives it a distinctly lopsided look. I keep stopping to admire the views through the window holes.

It is still wonderfully hot and cloudless. It is hard to imagine that it ever rained. I've always been strongly affected by the weather and fine, clear spells like this give me enormous energy. The heat, glare, and flies take some toll, but the sun's track is now low enough to throw tree shadows onto the building site for a lot of the day and that helps. Shade temperatures are quite cool.

I am still sleeping by the wharf but have moved off the logs to the lumber pile, for which I built a platform just the other side of the snag that Richard wants to eliminate. The dog is quiet and relaxed and the bear situation seems to have eased off. My eyebrow is mending; even the "black eye" is fading.

August 27, 1988

I am ready for the first tie log, the one that will join the three up-rights of the west wall. I have peeled and hauled it but will notch it in the morning when I am fresher and less likely to make a mistake.

The final section of wall, the one I had left open as a temporary

extra doorway, went up quickly; being weathered, the logs were comparatively light and easy to handle. They are a variety of tan browns
and silver greys. Part of the cut that makes the point of each filler is
visible; on the weathered logs this makes a sharp contrast of colour.
The lodgepoles are yellow and, if they have been beetle-killed, the
sapwood is bluish — I have yet to find out why this occurs. The
inner wood of the white-barks is a soft, pinkish tan. It is close-grained
because of its slow growth and, if it was only straight enough, would
make a very nice furniture wood.

The moon was full last night. It rides higher in the sky now and
is so bright that it makes two shadows; one from itself and the other,
ghostlike and higher, from its round reflection in the motionless
water. One feels at the centre of some strange celestial convergence,
or upon a different planet with two moons.

August 28, 1988

It was so hot at noon that I did something I never do — I lay down
for a short while after lunch. There was a thin, latticed shade on the
lumber pile by the wharf, and I was beginning to relax properly for
the first time since the bear attack at Sam's cabin. I had hardly
stretched out when,

"WOOF! WOOF! WOOF! WOOF! WOOF!"

A bear! A bear!

Where? Where?

Not more than four paces away was a large, upturned root tangled with dirt and rocks. Over the top of it poked two round, black,
bear's ears. I grabbed the bear repellant in one hand and a tin cup,
which I banged against the chain saw, with the other. Lonesome
barked magnificently. The two ears disappeared and, an instant later,
in a small clearing, I saw the bear properly. He looked at me for a
moment, then growled and ran off. It was not comforting to think
that he was now more interested in me than my food, but at least I
know for certain that it is not the trappers' bear that had followed
me, for the only black things about this animal are his ears and face.
The rest of his coat is a striking ginger colour. He is medium-sized
and I strongly suspect he is still young and only recently shoved out
into the big wide world by his mother, for bears are often very curious at that age. As long as he stayed only curious, I need not worry.

For all the trouble Lonesome has caused, her superior bear detector mechanism has more than earned her keep this last month.

But the bear's obvious interest in me has terrified me. Oh for the solid walls of a cabin. My nerves are wound as tight as rubber bands. Every cone the squirrels drop sounds like a footfall; every slap of water like a breaking stick.

August 29, 1988

The weather broke and I got wet on my lumber pile last night. Fortunately it did not rain heavily and today's strong wind should dry my sleeping bag.

I work in feverish haste. I raised both tie logs yesterday. One was unpeeled and it was so hard to skin I had to chip each inch of bark away with a draw knife.

All the ceiling joists are propped against the building, ready to be dragged up and notched over the tie logs. It will not be a pleasant job for I will be using the chain saw while balancing on top of the walls and will have to be up and down the ladder all day. I hope to fit them all tomorrow. It will be the last working day left before I have to go out again. The Bella Coola Fall Fair is to be held at the weekend; this gives me a chance to display a few paintings and perhaps sell one or two, a very welcome addition to my income. I am not sorry to be going out. I shall be glad of a chance to sleep between bear-proof walls. How I long for the day when I will have some of my own.

August 30, 1988

The ceiling joists are notched and nailed. A crude job, but I am too tired to care. I hauled the two plate logs and called it quits. The mountains are playing hide-and-seek in spectacular clouds.

I'm pooped.

CHAPTER 8

September 9, 1988

I left in the pre-dawn, anxious to try and make it to the ranch in one day in spite of the fewer hours of daylight. A rime of frost coated everything; the canoe was pale and slippery with it. I had prepared a thermos and a lump of bannock the previous night and I took them to the viewpoint behind Crescent Island, where I usually leave the canoe, and sat there and ate while I watched the sunrise. The lake was chill and misty. Vivid orange bands of colour came and went over the mountains.

The approach to Sam's cabin was, needless to say, somewhat nerve-wracking. I wore the imperfect glasses to give me as much distance vision as possible and going down through the swamps, the early sun was just to my right, blinding my single-lensed eye. I clutched the bear-repellant can as if it was a gamma death ray gun, but the only bear I saw ran off at once, as they usually do. A friend told me that when she had to walk through bear country, she used to sing to warn the bears she was coming. I didn't particularly want this bear to know I was there, but I warbled softly to the dog. I'm sure it did not charm the bears, but it did loosen my throat muscles sufficiently to enable me to breathe.

I did not stop at Sam's cabin but headed up the mountain side as fast as I could and was soon above the tree line. The flowers, which had been so spectacular such a short time before, were gone, burned up in the recent brief heat. It was the first time I had crossed the pass in glorious weather and, with the bear behind me, it was a wonderful trip.

I made excellent time. Not only because my bits of work had improved the route, but also because the swamps were drying out which made travelling faster.

The ranch was in chaos. Cornwall's mother, Barbie, and his sister, Ainslie, had arrived that afternoon along with several others in city casuals who all looked alike to my blurry vision. Boxes and crates were everywhere, spilling out of pickup trucks and trailers and jamming all the hallways of the house (which was a classic example of poor design, having all the windows at one end and a hopelessly gloomy kitchen at the back). Cornwall was racing about with a friend and a dog, and Ainslie, a lively, skinny kid of eleven, kept thrusting cats into my face and giving me their life histories. Their mother was small and fine-boned like the grandmother. She invited me to supper, but it was obviously not a good time to visit. Just before I left, a tall figure with shoulder-length hair, dressed in a bulky coat and cowboy hat, came into the ill-lit kitchen. This was the mysterious Alex. "The lover" seemed much younger than Barbie and I remember thinking, "What a wimpy-looking guy."

The Fall Fair was the usual fun and it was great to socialize with all my friends. I managed to win all the classes I entered and promptly spent the money on more nails. Most of my stuff was stored in a cabin down in the valley and it was there that I found another pair of glasses.

When I returned to the ranch, the family had settled in and I was more than glad to accept the supper invitation. Barbie was coercing delicious smells out of the black hole of the kitchen and, with the stove lit, it was warm in the cabin. And there was Alex, sitting at the light end of the room, no longer encased in the heavy outdoor clothing — and very obviously not a guy at all. She was a very well-shaped young woman.

I have lived in rural or isolated communities all my life and lesbians, or at least self-admitted ones, are a very rare species. I was immediately struck by Barbie and Alex's lively senses of humour. The second thing that impressed me was the large and copious library which crowded every available shelf, a wonderful array of literature, women's politics, and philosophy. Barbie and Alex will be my closest neighbours for as long as they last, sporadic invasions by the trappers excepted, and I think they are going to be a lot of fun. I drool over the library and have already slipped *Out of Africa* by Karen Blixen into my pack. I hope Barbie and Alex make out. Barbie grew up in the Peace River Country, but she has lived in the city since before the kids were born and they have never been out of it. They will have school by correspondence while they are here, although, periodically, they will go back to Vancouver to stay with their father. They all seem wildly excited at the prospect of their wilderness experience.

I left the ranch at first light and breakfasted at Cowboy Lake. The wind got up with the sun and, by the time I reached the pass, it was roaring and ripping through long, cold slabs of cloud.

I climbed higher than usual to see if there was a possible route to the lake along the ridge south of Whitton Creek, which would avoid the bears' prime feeding ground around Sam's cabin. Behind the ridge lay a high, treeless valley full of yet more lakes, which looked well worth exploring, but would take more daylight hours than I had at present, so I dropped down to the rock slide and picked up my usual trail. Every step brought me closer to The Bear. I bypassed Sam's cabin, waded the river, and began the slog up through the swamps. The sun was going down fast as I approached my lake, a golden ball that shot bright rays between the trees. The wind still roared. It was possible to canoe across the lake behind Crescent Island, but I simply could not buck the wind for the remaining short distance to the wharf. I beached the boat in the Second Inlet and completed the journey to camp on foot, every sense stretched to its limit. Had Ginger Bear been around while I was away? Is he waiting for me? But the dog was unconcerned and the camp was tidy and undisturbed. I almost wept with relief.

I spent the night in the tent. The wind dropped and in the morning I was able to retrieve the canoe. Bread is baking and at any moment I expect Richard with another load of supplies. In the Bella Coola Valley, which has a good growing climate, I was able to buy some locally grown, chemical-free vegetables, including a hundred pounds of excellent potatoes. I shall eat well for a while.

And when Richard has been, I will start work on the plate logs, which are the beginnings, at last, of the roof.

September 13, 1988

There have been some nippy frosts, followed by very beautiful days. The lake writhes briefly with mist while the pink and orange mountains float disembodied above it. The vapour soon burns off up here, but Nimpo is often fogged in until noon, which made Richard very late again the other morning. The fog hangs in the Atnarko Valley, too. Some days, when I lived there, I would have to climb far up the valley walls if I wanted to see any sun at all.

I cannot let these magical mornings fade without launching the canoe for a little while — the dog needs a run, after all. I have been much more solicitous towards her since her runaway, figuring that my neglect of her to that date was in a large part responsible for her behaviour. So I try not to think of the precious summer slipping by as I slide through the wraiths of golden mists and drift through the secret, shifting islands. When I come back to the wharf, the mist has gone and the sun is sharp and clear. It bounces off the minutely rippling water, sending a luminous network of quavering reflections over the trees and rocks of the point. My second cabin will stand in this spot. Will the flickers of light play over it, too? How quickly the warmth comes to this side of the point. My camp and building site are shadowed and they now remain cold until the sun is passed its zenith. Which is fine for working in but not very conducive to jumping out of bed in the morning.

This is blackfly weather. The first frosts seem to make these little bloodsuckers feed more. They tramp about in hobnailed boots on the edge of my hairline and where the ear protectors curve against my cheek. I tolerate them in silence. I have to curb my language now. Twenty miles from the nearest human being and I have to be careful of what I say because of a dog. Occasionally, if I inadvertently exclaim aloud at one of my mistakes, I immediately call in the direction of the camp, "Not you, Lonesome. I wasn't talking to you. Good girl, Lonesome."

Because the plate logs extend over the porch, they are twenty-three-feet long. Each one has to have seven notches to fit over the ceiling joists. I commissioned two thirteen-foot rafters to use as skids to slide the logs up to the tops of the walls. Once again the come along was pressed into service.

Richard brought the rest of the store-bought ceiling boards on his last trip. He'd loaded the same number as he'd carried the first time, but had been surprised how much heavier the plane had been. No doubt the boards soaked up plenty of water while they lay beside his wharf and I have not been able to provide a drier storage space here. They will have swelled with the water and are bound to shrink when they dry, but there is nothing I can do about it now.

I carried them from the pile by the wharf, three at a time. They are fourteen-foot shiplap, one-by-sixes in sawmill jargon, which, because they are planed, translates into five and a half inches by three-quarters. There is now a distinct trail among the rocks between the wharf and the building site, but it is much convoluted; manoeuvring the boards between the trees required a lot of body-twisting.

The first ceiling board needed to be fitted against the plate log but the rest followed in fine style. It is the only time that I have had a large chunk of obvious progress in a single day's work. How easy it would be to build a house if all the materials were machine-cut and to hand. Ninety percent of my work is finding, preparing, and, most of all, laboriously hauling the components.

It then occurred to me that it was high time to make the floor-boards to give them a chance to dry a little. The massive tree with the kink in it that I had earmarked for that purpose was not peeled and had dried very little since it was fallen. Most of the seasoning of the floorboards will have to take place while I am living on them. Because a great deal of shrinkage is inevitable, I will put the boards in upside down, then flip them over and finish them properly when they are dry.

The kinked tree had fallen between the cabin and the lake. Lumber-making creates enormous piles of fine-grained sawdust, quite different from the coarse chips produced by cross-cutting. I had no desire to have that unsightly mess in such a visible place, but the log was so huge that there was no way I could move it. It was all I could do to roll a section away from the top so that I had room to work the mill.

That tree fascinates me. The healthy way it was growing indicated that the kink had been initiated way back in the tree's history. I have been reading Malcolm Wilkins's *Plantwatching*. The sap-wood cells stay living in a growing tree, but the heartwood cells are programmed to die when their ends disintegrate so they form fine, immensely strong tubes to withstand the enormous pressure induced by transpiration. Consequently it is the heartwood that supports the tree.

But if it is only the heartwood that has strength, how did my kinked tree, which had virtually no heartwood left, survive countless winds and winter snows? How long would it have continued to survive?

I used a store-bought board as a guide for the Alaskan Mill to run the top slab off the log, then sliced off boards one-and-three-quarter-inches thick. They were so wide that my twenty-four-inch mill could barely squeeze through in places, but I will lose quite a few inches when they are edged. They were immensely heavy and difficult to stack. I placed scraps of wood between each layer to give them a better chance to dry, weighting the top one with rocks and stove-lengths so it would not warp too much. More stable lumber would be made by ripping the boards in half, but the width looks impressive and, by preserving it, I feel I have paid some kind of tribute to the tree.

September 14, 1988

Another day, another tree. I want access to a root cellar under the floor, which means that the boards that cover this part will have to be of cured beetle-kill so that they will not warp. I felled another lodgepole and have made lumber out of that one, too. The day was sunny and windless; the blackflies were out in force. I did not notice them so much when I was bent over the saw, but as I straightened up at the end of each board, my head hit a great cloud of flies. They don't seem to be biting much, but the crawling drives me crazy.

I was suprised to hear, in the spaces when the saw was silent, the "dik, dik, dik" of a robin. There were flocks of them, mixed with varied thrushes, constantly haranguing me with their alarms. I have seen neither species up here before. When I arrived in the spring, all sorts of birds were singing, but most were unfamiliar to me and by mid July they had all quit. At times, groups of small birds twitter back and forth apparently finding insects in the trees. The thrushes, however, must be after berries. The huckleberry bushes, which are so common in the dry ground on the rocky ridges, have born little fruit, but the crowberries are plentiful, as they seem to be every year in all alpine areas. They are tasteless and seedy to me (although I eat

them by the handful and spit out the pips: anything fresh is a treat), but the birds must like them and bears eat huge quantities. Which brings Ginger Bear to mind; I have seen no sign of him since I have been back. The salmon will be spawning in the Atnarko and perhaps all the bears are headed that way.

There is a new bird on the lake as well. It is a western grebe. It is similarly shaped to the loon, for it feeds in the same way, but it is much more dainty and fairy-like. It has an odd cry, a little mew like a cat.

The hummingbirds are long gone. I was very suprised to find any at all up here, but they occasionally buzzed around the camp and investigated my red gas cans. At Nimpo they were saying that both the hummingbirds and the swallows have gone so early it is bound to be a hard winter, but they always say that, every year.

September 15, 1988

I was able to pull the ridgepole up the skids onto the ceiling platform in the same way as I had lifted the plate logs, but I needed gin poles to raise it to the top of the end posts. I measured and notched the ridgepole, then tied the block and tackle to one end and the come-along to the other — and up it went. So there the ridgepole lies, pointing like a golden finger to the south, defining the shape of the roof.

And this momentous occasion must go unrecorded, for my camera has broken. It won't wind on. Goodness knows when I'll be able to get it fixed or replaced. Even at Nimpo, I am still hundreds of miles away from a repair shop; the camera will have to be shipped by mail or bus the next time I am out and I will not receive it back until the following mail trip.

I can't raise the porch rafters until I have something to stand on under that part of the roof. To make the porch ceiling I will need joists and before them the uprights at the end of the plate logs will have to be erected; and *they* can't be placed until the porch foundation is in. So I am back to ground level and have started at the bottom again. The porch foundation will be lower than the floor of the main cabin and about six inches away from it to give me room to pile snow from the ground when I want to bank the walls.

Another beautiful day; but how short they are getting. I am writing this by lamplight in the tent. There rarely seems to be much colour at sunset here — it is the sunrises that are so spectacular — but tonight was an exception. Pink paintbrush strokes of cloud were reflected in the mirror of the lake, unnoticed until I finished supper. Then I stood transfixed, toothbrush forgotten in my hand, until it faded. One moment my all absorbing thought was the current trivia, which at the time was the meat and gravy on my plate, the next, without warning, I suddenly became the tiny hub of the vast wheel of country that revolves around me. I feel strong and young, as if nothing can defeat me. At one and at peace with the world.

CHAPTER 9

September 16, 1988

It has snowed. Not just the few half-hearted flakes one might expect at this time of year, but a soggy, many-hour dump that has accumulated into two wet, sodden inches.

There was nothing particularly remarkable about the morning; it was a little gloomy, with clouds moving in swiftly from the north and the peculiar stillness that I have come to realize is common to winds from that quarter. Even when the first desultory crystals of snow floated down as I stood on the ceiling, drilling the ends of the diagonals that would brace the ridgepole to the end posts, I thought nothing of them. Then suddenly, fat flakes were whirling thick and fast. "It can't last, not at this time of year," I thought, not even bothering to go for my coat. But as I straightened from my work, the ground was already white; rocks, stumps, and brushpiles were taking on an unfamiliar look with colour gone and new and intricate details defined. And then it was half an inch deep on the ground and coming down thicker than ever. It was getting down my neck; dollops shook free from the ridgepole into my face as I whacked the nails holding the diagonals into place. The snow underfoot was becoming slick and dangerous; the roof was no place to be.

The chimney would have to be fitted as soon as the rafters were up, but to do that I needed the stove in place. That, in turn, needed the downstairs floor. When I had laid the joists I had flattened the tops roughly to give myself a less slippery surface to walk on, but they required considerable trimming before the floorboards could be laid, so this is what I tackled next, knocking out the excess with a heavy hammer and chisel. No longer was the cabin golden and airy; it was now a dark and dreary box through the ceiling of which the melting snow dripped copiously.

The snow did ease a little, but then the wind shifted back to the west and puffs of sodden sleet blew in through the window holes. I still needed more boards. The thought of going into the swamp and cutting them was less than enticing, but the alternative was to sit in gloomy misery in the tent for the rest of the day. I was unprepared for this weather. I had three pairs of boots with me, but the summer work boots were part canvas and they were instantly soaked, the seams of my hiking boots had been coming apart since I had tree-planted in them; even my rubber boots had a split across the top.

It is now supper time. Most of the ground snow has melted, but sleet and rain still alternate. I am crouched over the fire, shielding the flames with my body and feeling the warm smoke percolate through my clammy clothes. Mistily through the falling veils of precipitation is a curious greenish light towards the west. How beautiful it would be if I could view it from beneath a warm, dry roof through weatherproof windows.

Not one of my better days.

September 17, 1988

And yet today is so fabulous that my soul aches. It is sunny, sharp, and clear, but with that mellowness and melancholy that only fall can produce. A little snow fell again during the night, then froze white and sugar crisp onto everything. Rainbows of sparkles shone everywhere. Wolves sang in the forest.

It is afternoon now. The lake is without movement, the newly whitened mountains, blue-shadowed now that the sun has moved around, reflected in it darkly. Fish are jumping far out in the lake.

Their leaping bodies flash like meteors; the white splashes of water erupt soundlessly after them like distant, silent explosions.

September 22, 1988

My Indian summer was short-lived. It lasted only a day and the following one was as miserable as the one preceding it. It blew and sleeted, and ended by snowing enough to pile three more inches onto the ground. I cut more lumber and hauled the remaining rafters. The snow was stained purple with crowberries where I crushed them underfoot.

Inside the dripping box of the cabin, I laid the floor. First I shovelled out all the accumulated building debris, for any sawdust lying against the foundation logs will encourage damp and rot. Most of the sawdust I saved in boxes to use as insulation for the root cellar. This excavation, done before the ceiling joists were down, was now completely hidden in debris, and it had to be dug out again. Unfortunately, a floor joist goes right across the middle of it, which will be a nuisance when I want to put larger things into it, but there was no other place between the rocks where I could make a hole of any depth. It is not very big, but I will not need to store much more than three cases of jars and some potatoes. It is only temporary, for I plan on having a better one in the bigger cabin.

I defined the walls of the root cellar with bits of scrap lumber and piled the sawdust around it. There was not enough to complete the insulation and the remaining space up to the level of the floorboards was filled with batts of fibreglass. I will put more of these on top of the food in the cellar during the winter.

All that had to be done before the floor was laid, as there would then not be enough crawl space for me to get beneath the building. The dog could wriggle underneath and, in fact, that is where she has been spending most of her time for she hates wet snow even more than I do. But I have had to block her entrances because I do not want her to dig in the sawdust and either move it away from the root cellar or pile it against the foundations.

The wide, green floorboards from the leaning tree had dried very little and were almost too heavy to drag. I tied a rope to each one and shifted it a jerk at a time until it rested on the porch joists where I trimmed the edges. Inside, I jammed the boards as tightly as

I could but did not worry too much about the way they fitted, knowing they would all have to be done again when they dried.

The beetle-killed boards to cover the root cellar had still to be fetched from the swamp. They were much lighter, but the distance they had to be carried and the constant manoeuvring through the trees made the job just as tiring. Noticeable trails are being worn deep into the peaty vegetation of the swamp.

The snow stopped falling at midday and I shovelled what I could off the ceiling, but it was so sludgy it was difficult to shift. So all afternoon I worked inside in rain gear, poured on by drips, much wetter than I would have been outside.

The final board was the one against the back wall. It had to be cut short because, in the corner, a rock poked up just above the level of the floor joists. A covering slab was fitted over the hole; I plan to build shelves above it and the patch will hardly be noticed.

The following day was frosty and fine, but it was some hours before the sun cleared the trees enough to melt the ice on the building. But by afternoon, I could fit the three porch ceiling joists and tie a couple of planks over them as a temporary floor.

And finally, the rafters. The first one took a while to figure out, but soon I was fairly flinging them up and I finished them all in less than two days.

The strapping, or the home-made two-by-fours that would be fastened horizontally to the rafters to support the metal roofing, had all to be hauled from the swamp, nine journeys in all. Because the rafters were round poles, they were not completely even and the strapping had to be notched to fit. The bottom one involved leaning rather precariously over the side of the building to nail it down. As the layers of strapping grew higher, it became increasingly difficult to get both myself and the two-by-four through the grid that now covered the roof. Because the strapping was from trees of assorted lengths, I did not know quite how much I would need and there was not enough to complete the porch. But I will concentrate on the main part of the roof first and leave the delights of manufacturing more strapping for another time.

Metal roofing might seem a strange choice for someone who values the integrity of the wilderness. But shakes are out of the question, for there is nothing here from which to make them, and to buy them and fly them in would be far too costly and in any case ecologically rather ridiculous. So that leaves either metal or rolled roofing.

Rolled roofing would seem to be much cheaper by the yard, but it requires a solid layer of boards or plywood underneath it. From the ground, a roof looks to be a comparatively minor part of a building, but when you are up there working on it, particularly if it is a steep one, its true size becomes apparent. I have neither the trees nor the patience to make the lumber I would need to support rolled roofing and the cost of flying in either boards or plywood would make the whole roof more expensive than buying metal. I would not, however, condone galvanized steel, for from the air or surrounding mountains it would be an unforgivable eyesore. So I have paid for the extra cost of enamel; my metal roofs are dark brown. I hope this will make them as unobtrusive as possible. Metal has two further advantages: it is fireproof and it also sheds snow.

The sky has been clear all day, but there is a curious brassy look to the light and it has remained very cold. A solid wall of cloud, gilt-edged as the sun went down, has remained behind the mountains; I expect it is pouring with rain in Bella Coola.

I realize that, for all the longings for warmth and comfort of four walls and a roof, I am going to miss subtleties in the environment that can only be appreciated by living outside. I have spent several summers of my life without a roof over my head (usually in the southern hemisphere where there are fewer bugs) and I always feel uncomfortable when I first try and live between walls again. But this summer has been the coldest and wettest I have had to endure and I won't be too sorry for a house. Perhaps I'm forgetting past discomforts, or maybe I'm just getting old.

My supper is a disaster. It is fatal to try and write and cook at the same time. First I burned the curry powder, now the rice has boiled dry. I am having sardine curry tonight. I have eaten an enormous amount of sardines since I have been here. They are an excellent food, but I wish they were not so salty. Each can contains four headless, tailless fish. Somewhere on the other side of Canada I visualize rows of people, women probably, topping and tailing sardines all day and packing them into cans. Thank you, you women of the Maritimes!

September 23, 1988

More snow. It started just before daylight. It poured snow — there is no other word for it. I sat bowed over my breakfast fire in rain gear while the flakes hissed onto the stove top and melted on my pancakes.

Now that the strapping was in place I knew more or less where I wanted the stove, but the intervals between both the rafters and the ceiling joists had to be juggled to allow for the chimney. A plumb-line and an improvised pair of compasses made with a pencil and a bit of string gave me the mark in the ceiling for the chimney hole. While the snow plummeted wetly, threatening to obscure the pencilled circle, I cut out the disc with the little chain saw.

When the roofing metal had been packaged at the building supply store, its enamelled top had been protected by offcuts of galvanized steel. One of these, with the ridges bashed out of it, was prepared as a mat to put underneath the stove to help deflect both heat and sparks from the floor. By the time it was ready, a solid white circle of snow had appeared on the floorboards directly under the chimney hole, which was actually quite useful as it showed me the line of the chimney exactly.

I had found the stove in a store in Vancouver. It looks old, particularly now that it has rusted by sitting in the rain, but it is in fact a new one built with old castings. It is an upright parlour stove with a lattice of mica windows in the front doors. It seems to be a fairly good compromise between a heater and a cookstove. Its firebox is large enough to hold a fair amount of wood and yet its top has removable lids, thus allowing the right-sized pots to sit inside them and heat much more quickly. But its main attraction, for my situation, is that the doors, the top, and the little base with legs, all come off. In the store, even the body appeared to be in pieces, bolted together with shiny, very new-looking and somewhat incongruous screws. All this indicated that not only would I be able to lift the stove, but also there would be no difficulty getting it into and out of a plane. Richard had brought it to the lake on his most recent flight.

I fetched the base first, then all the bits and pieces: the doors, the top, and the lids. Richard, being much stronger than me, had swung the body of the stove in one piece directly onto my woodpile. I started to attack it with a screwdriver, then looked more closely at it and realized that the joints of the body had been sealed as well as screwed. Would I be able to break the seals without damaging the metal? How would I repair the seals if I did? I tightened all the screws again. If I stood above the stove body, I could just lift it off the ground; at a guess I'd say it weighed something over a hundred pounds. I've carried loads as heavy as that before, but that was stuff like flour which is dense and compact. And the trail between the wharf and the cabin, although short, was not only extremely rough and uneven, but also, at this moment, covered in a couple of inches of very slippery, wet snow.

I fetched my backpack frame, strapped the stove body to it, and sat against it on the lumber pile to slide my arms through the pack straps. I leaned forward to take the strain — and that is where I stayed. I could not budge. It was as if I was glued to the lumber pile. The stove's weight was obviously considerably increased by the leverage of its bulk. Now what? The snow slithered and rustled as it tumbled through the trees. I looked at the screwed and sealed joints again but I did not want to risk damage by breaking them apart. The sensible thing would have been to shelve the task until Richard came the next time; he probably would not mind helping me with the lifting. But once I get an idea in my head, I find it hard to let go. I wanted to fit the stove now. I would make one more attempt.

I have never made a greater physical effort in my life. Up wobbled the stove. The only way I could balance it was to stand with my body bent at right angles. My knees felt like jelly. And I had all those slippery, snow-covered rocks to negotiate. If I fell over, the brittle cast iron would break and probably my leg as well. It was the most foolish thing I have ever done alone in the wilderness.

I prefer not to think about that journey; I remember, in great detail, every rock and twist in the trail. Both the stove and I arrived at the cabin in one piece. Eventually, I lowered it onto the doorsill — and the rest was easy enough. But never, under any circumstances, is that stove going to be moved anywhere else again.

The section of government-approved insulated chimney that went through the ceiling was designed to be attached to heavy metal brackets to prevent it from falling though the hole. I shovelled the slush on the ceiling around until I found the box that held them, which I had put up in readiness the day before. The instructions were distinctly soggy. With a diagram, I can see at a glance what needs to be done, but I am not good at following written instructions. This disintegrating bit of paper informed me I would need various tools including gloves, safety goggles, and hard hat. I would also need a screwdriver, but of course it was different from the one I had already fetched for the stove screws.

Eventually, sitting there in the tumbling sleet, I understood that part of the brackets were to be bolted onto the top of the ceiling boards, and part screwed into a section of the chimney. The insulated chimney has a very thin outer skin and a layer of what seems to be asbestos between it and the flue. (There were no warnings about this in the instructions.) When I attempted to wind the screws into the outer skin, it simply bent. The screws were soft and they stripped in an instant. One or two went where they were supposed to, but I had to resort to nails for the rest. As the nails punctured the skin, grey asbestos dust puffed out. Some was also visible at the ends of the pipe sections. Hard hats and safety goggles would not give much protection against that.

I had three sections of the insulated pipe; the first was attached to the brackets and went through the ceiling, the second penetrated the roof grid, and the third reached well into the sky. The outer skin was very shiny and my marvellously distorted reflection glared froglike at me from it. A cap with a screen around it finished off the chimney. It seemed a little wobbly to me, although no doubt the flashing would help to hold it in place, but I anchored it against the grid with one of my trusty bits of wire.

Marrying the stove to the bottom of the insulated chimney was an enormously fiddly job and it took up the rest of the day. The snow has more or less stopped, but a bitter wind is blowing. I'm scribbling this in the tent, icy-fingered, squinting in the last of the light. A plane flew over as the clouds began to break. It landed and took off from the little lake above me and shortly afterwards I heard some shots. My trapping neighbours work for the outfitter who owns the hunting rights to the area; when I last saw them on one of my trips outside they mentioned they would be having a hunting party about now. There is a patch of feed for their horses not far from that particular lake and they often make camp there. Their clients fly in to meet them, so I will have neighbours for a few days. I heard a chain saw, too, although the camp must be six or seven miles away. They probably won't hear my saw unless the wind changes.

September 25, 1988

Euphoria! The first piece of metal roof is on! Too dark to see, too tired to write. Pray for a calm day tomorrow.

September 27, 1988

I was up when the stars were still shining. I had a couple of pieces of strapping still to fit and I worked on them feverishly, constantly sliding an eye to the sky, for the morning was both windless and snowless and, in view of the recent record, it was hardly likely to stay that way.

The small discrepancies that I was not able to eliminate on the ground have become exaggerated the higher the building has grown. So there was quite a variation in the lengths of the sheets of metal required from one end of the roof to the other. They were not too heavy, but I certainly would not be able to hold them in place and screw them down at the same time. So I had to devise a structure to hold them at the bottom until I had secured them, then trim off the tops. The support had to be absolutely square with the end of the roof or I would run into more problems. Up and down the ladder and roof grid I went with strings and a square. Finally I trimmed off the ends of the strapping, ran a board as a support for the edge of the metal along the gable end, and adjusted a system of boards nailed to the bottoms of the rafters as a support. It was not very strong and I did not dare put my weight on it, but I hoped it would hold the tin.

Amazingly, the wind stayed away. I fetched the first sheet from the wharf and propped it up on the windward side of the house. Up the ladder I climbed, squeezed through the roof grid, and hauled up the piece of roofing. My efforts with the square and strings had worked, for when the bottom of the tin sat on the baseboards, the edge ran exactly along the gable end.

My little home-made ladder was nowhere near long enough to

handle the roof; I could screw down the metal only if I could reach every part of it while perching on the roof grid. The problem was that I had to start the screw by bashing a hole in the metal with a nail. This took two hands and considerable force, involving a lot of body wrenching and twisting, yet another exercise in contortionism. But I was able to reach everything — just; how a shorter person would handle such an exercise I have no idea. I tied a string to a little open-ended wrench and whirled the screws down. The other end of the string was tied to my wrist, one less tool to retrieve from the ground should I drop it.

By the time that was done, the day was over, but it was with great satisfaction that I put the tools underneath the metal before I quit. If it snowed that night, they would at least stay dry.

The night was pale with moonlight and eerie with loons. The morning was calm again and four more pieces of metal went up before the wind rose and I had to quit. I hate being diverted from what I have set my mind to, but there were plenty of other urgent jobs. I found and prepared extra braces for the rafters. The wind became so fierce and cold that my numbed fingers dropped nails and tools and I was ready to weep with frustration.

This morning it was calm again, but under the overcast, darker whisps of cloud were flying silently in from the southwest, breaking off from a mass of gloom that hid the mountains. Gradually the nearer hills were swallowed up and I feared the worst, but all I got was drizzle. And it was even kind enough to fall unfrozen.

Today's first section of roofing was the one around the chimney, which required a lot of piecing and cutting and fiddling around. Then I found that the flashing that I had been sold was obviously not for a forty-degree roof as I had asked, but for a much shallower one. I am not in a very good position to deal with the incompetence of salespersons. The only thing I could do was attempt to butcher the one I had into some sort of shape. It is clumsy, but it will have to do.

When six pieces of metal were up, three to each side, I climbed astride the roof and fitted the first length of ridge cap. The shiny brown roof swooped steeply away on both sides of me and I tried not to think of the jagged rocks below. I thought I had done with the roof for the day, for the wind was increasing, but later it dropped again and the vague sun that glimmered faintly through the overcast showed me that I had at least two hours' daylight left, just enough time for three more pieces of metal (now that I had the routine down pat) and another length of ridge cap. I have now completely covered the main room of the cabin and the roof extends about two feet over the porch. The rest can wait. I will have to build a scaffold for the last piece of metal as then I will have no roof grid left to stand on; I don't want to spend the time figuring out how to build it at present. My next most urgent job is to fill all the holes in the walls: the windows; the door hole; and the gaps between the logs.

There are squalls on the mountains and rags of clouds are whipping by overhead, but the wind is not too bad down here. The last of the sunlight has a strangely metallic cast and it is glinting on a couple of ravens who are circling the camp in a rather odd manner. There are always ravens about, but they are never numerous and they generally keep to themselves. These two, however, are flying round and round not far above my head and croaking continuously. Their ragged black wings woosh as they flap them and their bellies gleam with a pewter sheen as they bank into the sun. Many peoples in the world attribute mystical powers to ravens and I cannot help but think of that when these two are evincing such unusual behaviour. It is almost like a warning: I hope they are not an omen.

CHAPTER 10

September 30, 1988 (I think)

Prophetic words! I cannot believe I wrote that! Those ravens heralded the wildest storm since I've been here, one of the worst, in fact, that I have ever lived through.

The day after the roofing covered the main room of the cabin, I worked away at the windows. The frames are sadly lacking the paint with which they were once covered, but it won't hurt them to stay that way for a while. I replaced a lot of the missing putty and levered out the rusty staples, which still held remnants of the brittle plastic film someone had used as winter insulation in the past.

Thin laths of wood had to be sliced from a board and nailed inside the framing to prevent the windows from falling outwards. The three panes that face the mountains will be fixed, but the others are designed to be opened. Instead of using hinges I made right-angled triangles and nailed them, bottom down and sloping side towards the windows, onto the bottom of the framing. This means the windows open at the top and lean into the room. To hold the windows closed, a loose triangle is wedged into the gap. I saw this idea on a barn once and thought it ideal for the cabin. On very hot days, the whole window can be lifted out to allow for maximum circulation.

The day had been rather cold and windy, but nothing out of the ordinary. The metallic glint persisted, however, and at sundown, a thick, black pall obscured the mountains. It looked as if more rain was in the offing; still, I had absolutely no concept of what was to come.

It was the wind that woke me. No ordinary gale this, for the trees were screaming. The night roared, the tarp thrashed and clapped, and the whole tent was shaking. It was raining heavily, too, driving with such force on the wind that it flew under the tarp, through the screen and clear to the back of the tent hitting me on the face. "My west windows," I thought. "They will never stand up to this."

Oddly enough, despite the heavy rain, it was quite light outside for the moon was just past the full and grinning like a demon through the flying spume. It hung high in the south so it must have been around one o'clock in the morning.

The windows were still in one piece, but I could feel them vibrate beneath my fingers as screaming gust after screaming gust slammed into them. In the howling dark, under the waterfall that cascaded from the newly created eaves, I battled with wind-wrenched boards. Working by the rain-slashed beam of a flashlight, I nailed them over the windows.

Inside the cabin, despite the absence of either door or chinking, the banshee wail of the storm was fractionally lessened. Perhaps I would have more chance of sleeping here than under the slapping, flapping tarp. In the roaring rain I fetched sleeping bag and foamy and tossed them onto the sawdust-littered floor. I lay rigidly awake, an unwilling listener to the lunatic symphony. There were new sounds in the background of it, the machine-gun roar of rain on the roof, the booming of the metal as the wind beat at the cabin, and a faint persistent drip that sounded suspiciously as if it was inside the building. And all the while the moon was bright enough to cast a discernible parallelogram of light through the door hole. It stretched and squeezed as it moved slowly over the floor.

When the door hole lightened with a greyness hardly brighter than the milky dark, the storm still raged. Walls of rain poured down and, to my despair, I saw that the roof was leaking in a couple of places. The rubber washers that fitted under the heads of the screws had obviously not all sealed properly. I had some roof glue, but there was no way I could get up there in this wind.

When fitting the windows, I had been cold enough to think about lighting the stove, but the consummation of a hearth should surely be a more solemn occasion than that of merely keeping warm. However, the desire for ceremony had evaporated suddenly. I hurried back to camp, past thrashing trees which I eyed with great trepidation, to retrieve an axe, frypan, kettle, and food, and a stove-length which I could split to find dry kindling. Half the tarp had ripped away. Inside the tent, in the depressions between the crowberry-covered rocks in which my body had lain, were puddles six inches deep.

A new stove, particularly one that is damp, takes a little while to coax into life. Smoke curled from the unsealed gaps, then suddenly the fire was away and red flames glimmered cheerfully through the latticed windows at the front. There was a strong smell of burning paint at first but the cabin was decidedly well ventilated with no door in the door hole or chinking in the walls, so the fumes soon dispersed. The warmth was wonderful.

I started chinking the west wall the moment I had eaten. The rain drove through the larger gaps, but one by one I sealed them off with fibreglass. Chinking is a slow job, but row by row, the gaps were filled. The south wall was next as that faced the wind, but the leeward side of the cabin could wait: the next priority was a door to fill the door hole.

I cobbled one together from store-bought lumber. The door hole, framed in logs, is, inevitably, not entirely square and the door needed a lot of lifting and measuring before it fitted. This would not have been such a problem were it not for the wind slamming under the porch with unpredictable fury. If I was holding the door when a gust came, the door acted as a sail and I was all but lifted off my feet. I tried to listen for the gusts, but coming over the lake they made no sound until they hit the trees, which were so few between me and the water, I had no warning. But the door is up — after a fashion. From the inside, I can see that it hangs outwards at the top, but for the present it fills the hole and I will adjust it when conditions are a little less inhibitive.

With every hole finally filled, the cabin became considerably warmer — and darker, especially with the boards up over the west windows. I chinked the last of the walls in the dusk, found a drier spot for my sleeping bags, and prepared to endure another sleepless night. Was it my imagination, or was the wind getting worse? Wham! came another gust. The trees screeched, the roof boomed, and the whole cabin shook like a rat in the mouth of a terrier. Could the building survive such treatment? Was this kind of storm normal up here? If my roof went, all my plans and hopes and scrimped wages would go with it. I jammed fingers into my ears to try and shut out the noise. It was that more than anything that was exhausting me so.

Another screamer, a crack, and a sighing thump. A tree that I had hoped to keep close to the porch had fallen. It had just clipped the edge of the roof. It rested so that some of its branches were jammed tautly against the kitchen window. So once again in the wild, moonlit dark, I worked by flashlight, carefully cutting away the branches. It was not raining at the time and the moonlight was brilliant. Fortunately, the window did not break. Perhaps my building was tougher than I thought.

When the moon was high, the wind began to ease a little, but by morning it was pouring with rain again and more water was dripping through the ceiling. I fetched disintegrating boxes of clothing, books, and toilet paper from the sorry-looking tent. Around the camp, twelve trees were down which astounded me, for I had not heard them go. A nice one behind the cabin that I had wanted to save for aesthetic reasons had been uprooted and taken two others with it. Near the camp, an ancient balsam had fallen and knocked down a beetle-kill. Further back, a smaller beetle-kill had snapped leaving a jagged, yellow snag like a broken bone. Another half-dead specimen had succumbed, one with hundreds of baseball-sized burls all the way up its trunk. And these were only the ones in my immediate vicinity. What did the rest of the forest look like? The only tree fit to use was the bigger of the three close to the cabin, and only a part of it was straight. The tangle of twisted trunks and roots has made a huge addition to my clean-up job, for they lie directly downwind of the chimney and will become a fire hazard when they dry out.

In the bottom of a hitherto unopened box of books (I could not bear the thought of being without them but had had no time to read) was a battery radio. I had not bothered with it until now, for in a large part of interior British Columbia, radio reception during daylight hours is usually nil; when the daylight hours are long, I am rarely awake in the dark. Reception is greatly improved, when it can be heard at all, by a peculiar arrangement of aerials, which I learned from other inhabitants of the Chilcotin. I had the pieces of it, and rigged it up in the torrential rain. An insulated copper groundwire runs from an aerial to a long spike pounded into the earth. The groundwire has to be excessively long so that the slack can be passed through a chink in the cabin wall then wound into dozens of fist-sized coils which are then taped to the back of the radio.

It is necessary to wriggle the coils around until you have found the right spot. Sometimes, the coils make very little difference to the signal, whether it is there or not, but at others it comes booming in with the coils and is non-existent without. For some reason, the rain helps the signal; on the day of the storm it came in so loud and clear that I had to turn the volume down. Thus the first item of news I had heard all summer was that the first space shuttle since the Challenger disaster had been launched and the Seoul Olympics were on. Then came reports of the tempest that had swept the whole northern part of the province, washing away bridges, blowing down power lines, and closing roads. One gentleman in Prince George, where many chimneys had parted company with their roofs, said it was the worst wind he had ever experienced in his seventy-odd years.

So I was not alone in my storm, and it didn't sound as if it happened all that often. And both I and my cabin had survived.

The clouds broke up during the afternoon, but it was still very blowy and unnaturally warm. I stood on top of the ladder and poked gobs of roof tar on every screw that I could reach with a long stick. The top ones would have to be done from the ridge, but I wasn't going up there until the wind dropped. It was bad enough on the ladder because no sooner had I braced my muscles for a blast of wind than I had to counteract them for the immediate and unpredictable vacuum that followed. The fallen tree that had clipped the porch made a suprisingly good scaffold for the east side of the house; I will leave it there until I have no more need of it.

As I dabbed away at the roof, I was suprised to hear a plane. Over the top of my cabin came the silver Beaver belonging to one of the float plane companies in Nimpo Lake. It moved forward very slowly, wobbling all the way and I shuddered to think what it was like up there in such turbulent air. It landed on the little lake above me and I remembered the party of hunters. What an ill-fated week they had had! Still on the ladder, I glanced up again as the plane flew back overhead. Above the ridge of my roof, leaning and lurching into the gale with narrowed, ragged wings, was a raven. He hung there for a while against the turbulent blue sky like a tattered, black flag. Was he saying, "I told you so"?

October 1, 1988

It is as benign and calm an evening as has ever existed. Pink, gentle clouds; a limpid lake; silence. My soul slowly unwinds. It is cautious about letting itself go, it watches every step and listens to every sound, uncertain of its freedom. The lake has risen a good six inches. The little animal with his secret hay pile by the firepit must be flooded out.

I have brushed out a trail between the cabin and the waterfront. The latter part was through a dense clump of balsam fir. I barged back and forth a time or two before deciding on the best route but, until I cut the trail, I did not see a most magnificent and monstrous stump that was hidden there.

Given a chance, the balsam fir will grow straight and tall like most conifers, but it can survive, in a dwarf form, in extremely exposed places, often fringing the windiest shores of a lake. Its attempts to grow upwards are foiled there, for its leaders are killed, but the lower branches, protected by the snow that drifts over them in winter, develop into sweeping tangled skirts, creating shelter for the vegetation behind.

The monster stump in the trail to the waterfront is ancient dead. Its trunk is only five-feet high, but it is half as broad and full of warts and bumps. Its three or four spindly leaders poke ineffectually skyward, but a great cage of branches sweeps around and down. A fantasy tree that is no less beautiful in death as it must have been in life.

I am going out tomorrow so have left the boards up over the west windows. I will build shutters for them eventually. I have tidied up the cabin: swept the floor; cleared years of other people's grime from the windows; and made a seat of planks and log rounds which, padded with my foamy, will double as a bed. Supper is cooking on the stove and a pile of dry firewood and kindling lies handy in the corner. It is hardly the grand entry into my new house that I visualized, but I am more comfortable than I have been in a very long time.

CHAPTER 11

October 11, 1988

As I launched the canoe into the glass-still, morning lake, the mountains already fiery with dawn, it suddenly occurred to me that this would be a good time to try the Avalanche Lake route to the road. This is another branch of Whitton Creek which starts just beyond a very small rise east of the cabin and which meets the river about half way to Charlotte Lake. The map indicated that, both from its length and the number of lakes, it might be a better winter route than the one I had used before; I preferred to try it before the snow flew so I would have a good idea what to expect when travel conditions became less forgiving.

The weather proved as fabulous now as it had been miserable before. The air was sharp and golden with the clarity of fall in full swing. Frost nipped the shadows and the underbrush; the huckleberry, willow, and especially the mountain rhododendron were ablaze with reds, bronzes, and gold. For most of the day there was not a breath of wind and the lakes were soundless as dreams. The cones that the squirrels bit off the trees made sharp cracks in the sun-drenched stillness. When the breeze did start, it ruffled the water to a deep ultramarine almost hurtful to the eyes against the orange gold of the surrounding slough grass. On Avalanche Lake itself, the great snow chutes, which plunge clear to the water's edge, were clothed with aspens whose pale, etherial flames are surely one of the most beautiful of all the fall colours.

A feast for the senses it certainly was but as a hike the route was a dead loss. The embryonic beginnings of the river trickled down a steep-sided gully and there, where the choice of direction was limited, I ran into a few old blazes left by some long-gone trapper; there was little indication on the ground, however, that any human had ever passed this way. The blazes were high on the trees, testament to the depth of the winter snow. As with the other trap trail, they followed the winter path of least resistance, which meant bog, bog, bog. The recent deluge had filled these to overflowing so that I was often up to my knees, once for almost two miles at a stretch. Lonesome usually carries a good chunk of my gear as well as her own food but her pack had to ride on top of mine while the miserable dog, who loathes water, splashed and swam behind.

Winter travellers use ice; now that the water was open I had to scramble round the lakes where trails were non-existent and choked with wearying windfall, much of it new after the recent storm.

It does not matter which way I go to the road, I always have at least one river to cross. This crossing was close to the junction of the two rivers which were swollen and roaring and would have been quite a problem had a fallen tree not spanned the deepest channel; the remainder was not difficult to wade.

I was benighted long before I reached Charlotte Lake and had several more hours hiking to do before walking across the beach at Rimarko. The new route had not saved me any time at all but it was another piece of country satisfactorily under my belt.

I had a good visit with Barbie and Alex and the kids. They were full of talk of the storm but, apart from a few trees down, they had had no serious damage. The cabin they are occupying has big, plate glass windows at the lake end and was never designed for winter living. A previous caretaker has stuffed pink, naked fibreglass batts under the ceiling but the floor and ill-fitting doors are full of draught holes. Charlotte Lake seems to be in a rain-shadow; it gets half the precipitation even of Nimpo. So there is usually not a lot of snow and what falls flies away on the wind, leaving nothing with which to bank the walls.

It is natural to speculate as to how newcomers, particularly city folk, will survive their first winter in this country. I've no doubt my somewhat esoteric plans were treated with equal scepticism by anyone who gave me a passing thought. But, frustrated and terrified as I often am, it has never occurred to me that I couldn't somehow make it work. I suppose that is the key to all endeavours: if you think you can do it, you can.

My decision to be a wilderness dweller was not spur-of-the-moment; the idea grew gradually. My father, a Polish refugee in England, started a woodworking business making furniture and restoring antiques. So I played with wood and tools as a child; my mother made almost everything that my father did not and so, without being conscious of it, I learned independence of the system. However, in my experience, all houses were built of brick or stone and the idea of constructing one never entered my head. That was one of the few things that Other People did.

The place I grew up in was (then) quite rural. I have never lived in a town or city. Even my college was an agricultural one and surrounded by fields and farms. I was always both a loner and a compulsive walker and have always been fascinated by nature. These attributes were the foundations for expeditions that grew more ambitious and encompassed country that became wilder and more rugged as the world began to open before me. In Australia I first experienced the euphoric "high" of being alone in the bush for several days: in New Zealand I developed mountain skills. There, also, I met North Americans who made me aware that the art of cabin building was still alive and well, something I thought had died out with Jack London.

People are always asking me why I live the way I do. There is no "why." I like the idea, opportunities have come my way, and so — why not? I am not "sacrificing" the outside world — far from it. I am well aware that I am inexorably linked to it and no less dependent on it than anyone else. I do have the enormous satisfaction of choosing what I want from it. The material things like televisions and washing machines, which most people take for granted and which, for some perverse reason, are used to measure our "standard of living," have never been as important to me as my surroundings. This is not righteousness but simply something that is — whether I have genetics or upbringing to thank for that I have no way of knowing.

Not that I would reject such conveniences if they were readily available. If hydro went past the door I would plug into it: if plumbing came miraculously into the house I would be delighted to have hot water at the turn of a tap. But these things are either logistically too complicated or expensive — or inseparable from having close neighbours. Not that I dislike people, far from it. I have wonderful friends. I simply don't want to live within sight or earshot of them. I need space.

And silence. Most people seem to tolerate a lot of noise. But for my first two years in Canada I inhabited a converted sauna in a rural area close to Salmon Arm, B.C. I was two miles from the Trans-Canada Highway and could just hear it. It was always there, on the edge of my consciousness, and it drove me crazy. Perhaps the combination of a non-electric house and living alone exaggerates sensitivity to noise, but I love to hear the quiet and tiny sounds of nature.

The words "remote" and "isolated" to describe my way of life are city conceits. "Remote" means "apart from" and I am indeed apart from the city and other people. But I am very close to nature and the way the world functions; in this respect it is city folk who are remote.

I need people just as much as anyone else. Not only indirectly, such as those who grow my flour and manufacture my gas and chain saws, but as people to socialize with, to talk to, to discuss issues and tell them what I'm doing. Also, on a practical scale, it is very handy for a wilderness dweller to have an outside contact whom he or she can use to deal with things like mail, and to store such stuff as is impractical to take home. When I lived on the Atnarko, my "home from home" was in the Bella Coola Valley. Now it is with Gloria and Roger Folsom who run the Wilderness Rim Resort, one of six outfits catering for fishermen on Nimpo Lake. I have known Gloria and Roger for so long now that I tend to take them for granted. They have four kids and several grandchildren but no matter how full the house is there is always space made for me. Gloria and Roger have been at Nimpo for fifteen years and they love the place. Their temperaments are better suited to the twenty-four hour day, seven days a week job of running a resort than mine; my visitors, if I ever get that far, will be in small groups at spaced intervals so I will have a completely different relationship with them.

The eyebrow incident made me think a little more about the possibility of an accident. I always give Gloria and Roger my estimated date of arrival as a safety backup and am careful never to be

late. But that would not be a great deal of help should I seriously
injure myself long before I was due out. So I thought it a good idea
to speak to the local pilots who flew so often over my head and
arrange a signal should I need help. The ground-to-air symbol for
"require medical assistance" is a large cross; I could make one with
the ripped blue tarp on the little swamp to the north of me. After
telling Richard, I went to Stewart's Lodge, the oldest resort on the
lake, which also runs an air charter service.

The current generation of Stewarts are Duncan and Rhonda.
Duncan was out flying but Rhonda was at the desk.

Rhonda, of course, had heard of my doings. She wanted to know
all about my place. Where was it? How was I making out? What did
I call it?

I have long puzzled over this last question. Nothing has presented itself as a name. The trapper calls it "Square Lake" (for what
reason I can't begin to imagine). I want to bill my business as "an
Alpine Experience." "The Square Lake Alpine Experience" hardly
has the right ring to it.

Sam Sulin was the original trapper; his brother is still alive and I
visited him hoping he might have known what, if anything, Sam had
called the lake. But there are so many unnamed lakes in this country
I was not at all sure the old man understood my description, which
was vague at best, having very few known landmarks on which to
hang it. This country was never lived in by the Indians. It was visited
occasionally for food gathering but there were far better hunting
grounds elsewhere.

The wind, particularly the west wind whose power was still very
fresh in my mind, had very much formed the character of the lake.
But "Windy Point" or "West Wind Lake" sound so banal. I mentioned to Rhonda that I would like a local Indian name, if there was
such a thing, as a mark of respect to the people of the area. She at
once lifted the phone and talked to a native teacher who taught the
Carrier language at the Anahim school.

Many Indian words are difficult for white people to pronounce,
but the translation for "West Wind" is "Nuk Testli." The "u" is short as in
"but" and the "t" is silent; to make it sound right for white people I
would have to misspell it. Nuk Tessli. "The Nuk Tessli Alpine Experience." I'm not sure if it is what I want and I have a little time to
change my mind, but if I am going to solicit business by my third
summer, which is my intention, I will have to have a brochure printed

by next year and will need to settle on a name before then.

Before I left, Rhonda suddenly asked me if I wanted a forequarter of goat which hung in their meat safe. The hunters who shot it wanted only the trophy. I am never one to refuse a free meal. As it would have been impractical to carry it home (both because of its weight and its attractiveness to bears), I took it to Rimarko and shared it with Barbie and Alex. It had been hanging for several days and was prime and most delicious to eat.

My taste of new country on the way out to Nimpo had whetted my appetite for more. So instead of following Maydoe Creek up its west side, I crossed it near the foot of Cowboy Lake and headed for a shallow pass in the long, bumpy ridge to the south. I hoped that, by crossing it, I would find a way into the high valley I had glimpsed from the top of the big rock slide the last time I had hiked home.

Either I had left Rimarko later than I thought or the ridge was further than it looked, for the day was ending long before the pass was within my reach. It had been hot and the rocky slope above the tree line was devoid of water so when I found a tiny creek, almost soundless and barely a hand's breadth in width, I made camp for the night. The low rays of the setting sun turned the hills about me to russet and rose; the leaves of the huckleberries were so intensely red they seemed as disembodied and unreal as discarded, painted fingernails. The light from the luminous sky was reflected in the lakes I had left behind; they lay like limpid beads in the dark cradle of the shadowed forest below. I stretched out on a tentless bed of crowberry beneath stars that pricked, then twinkled, then shimmered and danced across the heavens. There was a good frost during the night.

My airy perch was shady in the morning and very cold. The ridge ahead was gold-rimmed by the sun. The scrubby willows and dwarf birch underfoot were rimed with frost and, now that I didn't need it, there was plenty of water. It seeped through the broken seams of my boots and turned my toes to ice.

The last thing I expected was to encounter another human being. But there was a sudden rattle of a horsebell and a whinny. In front of me, on top of a small rise, a figure was abruptly drawn against a golden aura of sunlit smoke. It bore the unmistakable beat-up hat

---

worn by Bob Cohen, my trapper neighbour. "Put the coffee on, it's Chris," I heard him say. I came over the rise into sun and warmth and the sweet smoke of the fire.

Bob is as much a feature of this country as the wind-bent trees that sprout from the rocky soil. He has been in and out of it since he left school, which must be upwards of thirty years ago, and his childhood in Alaska encompassed a life not so very different. He is small and wiry with grizzled hair and close-cropped beard. The hat looks as though it first saw the light of day when Bob himself first came into the world.

Francie Wilmeth, his partner, came to Anahim Lake thirteen years ago to help her archaeologist father do some research. She met Bob, found (as she puts it) "that Bob had the best pack-horse string in the country," and that, for her, was that.

Son Patrick made his entrance five years later in the middle of trapping season. Bob and Francie use a cabin at Rimarko Ranch for a winter base. During Patrick's first year, Francie trapped close to the cabin while Bob toured the back of the line. Since then, the boy has been taken everywhere, travelling by snowmobile in the winter and on horseback in the summer. He has his mother's colouring but is otherwise a clone of his father in every detail, right down to the shape of his hat. One puzzles as to how someone of such tender years could have redesigned a piece of headgear so drastically.

Many people condemn those who wish to rear their children away from towns and schools. They cite: "lack of learning experiences" and "an inability to relate to others." They actually feel sorry for them when they are brought up differently from themselves.

I have known many children whose only education has been by mail, radiophone, or even parents alone: providing the parents care I have yet to see a child who has suffered from it. There have been cases where bush-reared children have been neglected, just like in cities, but that is the law of averages, not circumstance.

Like a great many wilderness dwellers, Bob and Francie read well and copiously. Patrick already has a passion for books far beyond that of most kids of his age. And one could hardly call the boy shy or inarticulate — given half a chance he chatters like a whiskeyjack. At eight years old he can handle a horse and an axe better than most grown men. His discipline is that of the country and the country does not readily let him make mistakes. Is Patrick really suffering by not learning how to punch his buddy in a hockey game, or gang up on street corners and fool around with dope? Whatever he may eventually do with his life, it will be for reasons of his own and not because of peer pressure. He has learned what many people never do — to think for himself.

Bob and Francie were on their way out to Rimarko, having finished a month-long trip guiding hunters and stocking their trapping caches with firewood and food. Three of the latter had been broken open by the bear, no doubt the same one I had encountered at Sam's cabin.

Talk inevitably gravitated to the big storm. Their camp had been in a more sheltered location than my cabin but it had been very uncomfortable. Four clients had flown in on the plane I had seen; they had spent the bulk of their trip playing poker in a sodden and gloomy tent. For that privilege they had paid $25,000 between them and all they had shot was one goat.

"One goat?" I said, the wheels of my brain clicking into gear, knowing that the plane that had flown them in had been Stewarts'. "What did you do with the meat?"

"No one wanted it," said Francie. "They only wanted the head and skin. They would have left the meat there but we shipped it out as we knew someone would eat it. It's not as though there was no room on the plane. Besides, if too many carcasses are left in the bush, predators increase their litter size and after a while an imbalance of nature is created."

The goat had to be the one whose leg Rhonda had given me. The meal Barbie's family and I had enjoyed so much at Rimarko had been worth exactly $8,250!

Armed with fresh information about the route I intended to take (including Patrick's detailed description of the "best patch of blueberries you've ever tasted in your life") I slowly finished climbing the ridge. Below me appeared a clutch of new lakes, the largest of which was Fish Lake, so popular as a fly-in trip for fishermen. It was almost at the headwaters of its stream; it is thought to have been unofficially stocked at one time but the size and number of the fish that exist there are nonetheless a mystery.

If I crossed the barely noticeable watershed at its head and continued north I would drop abruptly down another creek and eventually tumble into Banana Lake. But I turned west, climbed a little again, and was now in the high, treeless valley for which I had been aiming. If the drop off towards my lake at the other end of the valley was feasible, it would be a good alternative route to the bear swamps.

It was a pleasant stretch of hiking, being open and full of creeks and yet more small lakes. It is unusual to find alpine country so well endowed with water. An old game and horse trail cut through wetter places and here the fresh tracks of Bob and Francie's string were visible but otherwise the rocky ground hid the marks of the shod hooves well. The trail petered out at the end of the valley which culminated in a wide plateau with a magnificent view of the Coast Range. I could not see my lake, but the familiar shapes of the peaks that surrounded it pinpointed its location.

Now the land sloped downwards. Once I hit trees, I was running without landmarks, but the bush was fairly open and full of frost-burned, golden swamps that were now dry and grassy rather than brushy and quite easy to walk over. I knew that, sooner or later, I must hit the stream that joined my own river between Sam's cabin and my lake.

This stream was in fact a wild torrent that roared green and white-toothed in a sunless gorge. It took a while to find a crossing place and as this is the time of year when the water was almost at its lowest (for the floodwaters from the storm have now drained away), the prospects of crossing during the spring and summer high water do not look too good. Bob and Francie have never gone down the gorge as it is too rough for horses; in any case their destinations require a different direction.

After the gorge the country dropped very steeply into thick brush, another area I shall have to find a better way around if the high valley route is to be workable. I crossed my own river in the last of the light and, with eyes and ears fine-tuned for bears, arrived home at dusk. Everything was as I had left it: the browning brushpiles; the lopsided door tied with string; the note of my whereabouts pinned to it in the unlikely event that anyone came. I threw a fire into the stove, fetched a bucket of water from the lake along the newly cut trail, unearthed some canned meat and potatoes from the food crate by the camp, and started supper. Then, before I sat down, I wrenched the storm boards off the front of the cabin to let the evening light into the room. How beautiful was my lake, calm and green in the afterglow, between the dark masses of land.

Chapter 12

October 14, 1988

These tranquil, golden autumn days seem as if they will go on forever, but I know that I can't afford to waste them; it was with great reluctance that I forced myself back onto the roof.

For the final two sheets of metal covering the porch I had to come up with some kind of scaffold. As always, time spent on such extraneous projects was begrudged and safety was somewhat compromised. With boards lashed to the porch ceiling joists with quantities of rope I constructed a somewhat precarious walkway jutting beyond the end of the roof. I could reach all but the top two screws from it; the inverted washtub with a bucket on top supplied the balance. It was a very insecure perch which was really rather stupid but it worked.

So the roof is on, every screw dabbed with roof tar for good measure. I have put extra screws along the edges of the roof to give it more strength in the event of another violent storm and have used precious boards to line the underside of the porch roof, as that is where the wind hits the metal most severely.

I have pretty well completed the move inside. There is now a work bench below the kitchen window and a built-in table beside the door in the south wall. Buckets and planks have furnished me with a temporary bookcase along the north wall; when I refurbish the cabin I will build another sleeping bench there.

The balmy weather and the comfort of the logs around me makes me lazy. No longer do I have to rush to work in an effort to get warm. I read, something for which I have had little time during the summer, and must tear myself guiltily away from the books. How wonderful it would be to just sit and enjoy the place. But there is so much still to do. The shell of a building is the easy part; it is all the finishing that takes the time.

I have hauled everything over from the camp: the rest of the tools, a bale of insulation, the battered tarp and tent, and the garbage cans and the food from the crate. Some of the latter has gone straight into the root cellar, but the majority will eventually go upstairs when the attic is usable. That will be my next major project. The floor of the attic has to be done first; this involves constructing a framework to hold the insulation, fitting the insulation itself, and finally laying the floorboards, most of which I still have to make. Then there are the gable ends (more boards to cut) and the windows to fit into them, the door to construct, and the ladder that will give access to it. Both upper and lower porches have to be floored and the floorboards made for them as well. Within a couple of weeks I could well have the first real fall of snow; all the outside work must be done beforehand, for I will not be able to find materials once the snow lies deep.

I am writing this by lamplight: the sky is black beyond the windows. There is going to be another frost tonight. The sun set in a clear, orange sky that turned to apple green behind the mountains. I have brought the saws and chain oil can inside for the oil almost solidifies these cold mornings.

After the sun went down, a crescent moon three or four days old appeared among the lattice-work of the trees to the south. It stayed close to the horizon and swung slowly over the lake, pulling a trembling spear of light in its wake. As the moon set, a chunk was bitten off it by the south ridge. For a while, only its upper half was visible, peeping over the shoulder of land, glowing like a monstrous, neon tooth.

October 20, 1988

The morning sun has touched the mountain peaks with pink. It flushes deeper, then burns to orange, then gold, then yellow and cream, then white. There is a pause before long golden fingers of light flood through my eastern window.

There has been another windstorm. This one lasted only a few hours but a couple of gusts were as violent as anything that occurred before. The wind ran through all the western points of the compass, starting in the northwest, where it was noisy, but a little cooler and more stable; then west and a little more boisterous; then southwest and suddenly very wild and growing warmer all the time. This happened just at daylight and I was about to rush out to nail up the storm boards, not yet having made the shutters, when the wind swung visibly in a matter of seconds further to the south and was suddenly stilled. The clouds were racing overhead with no less speed; I can only assume that the topography of the land, although not particularly high in that quarter, must deflect the wind when it comes from that direction, just as it seems to do when the clouds stream in from the north.

The worst of the gusts come straight from a gap in the horizon, the lowest part of all the land that surrounds me, immediately south of Mt. Monarch. It must be one of the major holes in the Coast Range and its effects are further exaggerated by the height of the mountains that surround it. It coincides with, or perhaps has caused, a natural gap in the vegetation along the waterfront so that the cabin is in a bit of a wind tunnel. This was something that I never bargained for when I chose the site, but I'll simply have to live with it. I would very much like to know what wind speeds are attained here. Although it can give me no actual figures, I have an indicator of sorts — the glass in the south window. It is extraordinarily elastic and it flaps in and out as the gusts hit it. Its mobility can be measured by whatever is reflected in it, most particularly the lamp that sits behind my head on the north windowsill. Even when boards are over it (for I have felt obliged to cover this window, too) the reflections still waver considerably. Unfortunately, it is an odd-sized window and cannot be moved from there. But perhaps its fluidity has saved it, for it was not protected in the major storm; sitting on the floor, I was not in the right position to notice its movement.

Boards, boards, and more boards. Day after day, I fall trees, set up the log for the mill, and slice and slice and slice. My big saw stumbles on; it is no more happy than I am at performing this task. I have been told that the carburettor adjustments have to be altered considerably at this altitude; I have been fiddling with them and have certainly changed the sound of the saw, but have not improved its performance. But I really can't complain about that saw. I have lost a multitude of nuts and bolts, forgotten to clean filters (there are three altogether), cursed and sworn at it, and like it no better than when I first pulled its starter cord, but in a perverse sort of way, I have to admire it, for it has nursed me through a lot of growing pains and given me very good service.

It took four trips to haul the two-by-fours needed to support the attic floor. They were already crusted with frozen snow. My cabin has been adapted to its natural materials and environment rather than bullied into the standard measurements of the building industry and the two-by-eight-foot sheets of styrofoam insulation had all to be cut to fit. (A Beaver can carry a two-by-eight-foot sheet inside it, a four-by-eight has to be strapped outside; not exactly practical for styrofoam.) With a kitchen knife I poked fibreglass into every crack; I remembered how when I used styrofoam at the Atnarko and neglected to chink the cracks, the draughts whistled through. I preferred styrofoam for the floor as any liquid spilt on it would not harm it — and with the more modern compositions these days, using styrofoam is probably not much more abusive to the environment than anything else.

Then the floorboards, carried one by one from the swamp. These are all beetle-killed and I hoped they will not shrink too much so I have fitted them properly right away. Although they were edged in the swamp, they still needed adjustments and I ran a chain saw between them a time or two where necessary. It is suprising how much of the sawdust has worked through into the main room below. At the end of each day I find fresh little lines corresponding to the gaps in the ceiling boards, all over the tables and my sleeping bag.

Needless to say, there were not enough boards in my first estimate, and I had to go back into the swamp and fall another tree. It is getting harder and harder to find anything worth using and the boards are getting narrower. Some have quite a twisted grain and are inclined to split, but I'm putting those at the edges where the lowness of the roof will prevent any traffic and eliminate stress on them. I have amassed a pile of assorted shorter boards. It is impossible to calculate exactly how many I will need for the gable ends, for I will not know where the diagonal cuts will come on them until I start to fit them. The north gable end will have two small windows in it, the south will have a hole for the door. The window framing has to be held in place with extra uprights that I have yet to find; the inner shell will be constructed of bought boards, but I don't have those yet. As long as the outer gable ends are fitted, particularly the north one that is not protected by the porch, the worst of the weather can be kept out of the attic.

October 23, 1988

Gale upon gale upon gale. Roar-boom! Roar-boom! I lie in the dark and listen to it. It rained heavily yesterday and the forecast is for more today. But at the moment the sky is clear and leaping rags of clouds are flying past the stars. I used to exult in the wind, but the constant battering I am receiving here is wearying. I turned the radio on to give myself something else to think about, but it did not help. In Bangladesh, hundreds were killed when a ferry was capsized in a typhoon. Hurricane Joan is devastating Nicaragua with winds to 200 kilometres an hour — our fiercest gusts, according to the weather office, are less than half of that. I cannot imagine the terror that must prevail; there would be nowhere to get away from the storm.

Closer to home, in the Fraser Valley, a supermarket roof has collapsed ...

CHAPTER 13

November 14, 1988

It is close to the time when I must go out for mail again — hard to believe that it is nearly five weeks since I dined on the $8,000-plus leg of goat at Rimarko.

My world is different now for we have had our first permanent fall of snow; fortunately, it held off until I had fetched everything that was needed from the swamp. The gable ends are filled in, both upper and lower porch floors are done, and the shutters for the down-stairs windows have been made. I have run out of nails and store-bought boards, so cannot start to line the attic or build an upstairs door, but the overhang of the porch protects that opening from the weather fairly well. It doesn't keep the squirrels out, though. They made havoc of my cardboard boxes when they were stored outside and I now hear them galloping about upstairs and chewing busily. Almost everything not immediately needed is up in the attic out of the way. There is no permanent ladder yet; my building ladder will suffice at the moment. It can be taken down when I go out so that bears (if there are still any about — there has been no sign of them) will, I hope, be discouraged from climbing into the attic. A trapdoor has been made to fit the ladder hole in the upper porch floor; I can just reach it by standing on the dog kennel which now takes space on the porch. Lonesome would rather stay in the cabin by the stove, but there are many miles of winter travel ahead of us; she will grow a better coat if she is forced to stay outside. However, when the southwest wind screams across the porch, I take pity on her and bring her in. Not that we've had bad winds since the beginning of the month. There have been the usual gales one might expect at this time of year, but the shutters have hardly been needed, although I put them up if the weather looks rough in the evening so that I am not faced with the prospect of having to get up in the middle of the night.

The firewood was a job of some urgency. Each stove-length has to be manhandled one at a time, or at best, two or three at once on a pack frame. A wheelbarrow would be hopeless on these rocks. Some of the wood has been piled on the porch, but much of it lies in loose heaps scattered around the property. I bring in a little at a time so it does not seem so dreary a task. It will not be enough to last for all the time I plan to spend here this winter, but there are several standing beetle-kills close to the cabin which I have deliberately left so that they can be cut down as required; they will stay drier and be far easier to find that way.

It was a little odd to suddenly find myself at a comparatively loose end when the nail supply terminated. My constant conscious thoughts since I first set foot on the place have been for the next task at hand. I feel a little unbalanced, as I did when the wind gusts slammed into my body, then suddenly left me in a vacuum.

Canoeing was my first indulgence. When the wind gods were kind, I explored the lake from end to end, enjoying all its nooks and crannies, rocks and trees, sunrises and sunsets, and its many lovely moods. One morning I paddled to the back of Crescent Island and was suprised to find new ice behind it. It had formed as mats of feathered fans, all swirled and interlocking like a million beating birds' wings. The canoe could break it easily. But soon thicker, stronger ice began to grow around the edges of the lake and I could no longer launch the canoe. I overturned it onto the platform that had held my lumber by the wharf. Now, even if I'd had the money to buy more lumber and nails, a plane would not be able to bring them in. Not that anyone is flying out of Nimpo now. The Stewarts are gone for the winter and Richard takes his float planes out of the water at the end of October. As soon as the ice is good enough, which will not be until late December, he will fit a plane with skis.

I have been exploring the country on foot as well. A little way beyond the swamp just north of me is a small creek. Even though the plants are ravaged by the wind and frost, I could see that a different ecology existed there, partly because of the shelter in the little gully, and partly because of the damp. The spruce that tangled the bottom of the gully was hard to push through in places, but when a trail is brushed out along the creek, it will make a pretty walk. There are two small lakes not far up the creek and a couple of tiny meadows.

One day, before the snow came, I crossed the creek and plodded up the steep, rocky ridge beyond. As I climbed higher I could see tantalizing glimpses of my lake and the expanding mountains, but mostly the forest hid the view. There were places where the rocks were as big as houses and jumbled into steeply sloping piles. Finally, there was a bluff (with an easy way up around the end) from whose naked top, the view was wonderful. My lake was spread below. The cabin was behind trees and invisible from the lookout, but the point and all its surrounding islands were plain enough. It was a dullish, windy day and the blue-grey lake was edged in white as the waves creamed against the rocky shores. To the west, an impressive chunk of Coast Range was vaguely visible, although the weather hid most of it, and to the east were the two newly discovered lakes up the little creek. To the south, behind my lake, lay a great panorama that encompassed the first half of my route to the road. The swoop of the valley of Whitton Creek was plain to see, and the big rock slide where my trail climbed out of the valley and over Maydoe Pass, all solidly white now with the approaching winter. Further west was the cut that housed Fish Lake; the twin hills to the right of it flanked the high valley that I had followed on my last hike back to the cabin. I could pick out the gorge where I'd waded the rapids and I looked and looked at the wintry country around it, trying to see with x-ray eyes and penetrate the distance and the trees. But, from this far away, everything looked flat and easy. I could just make out the sheen of two more lakes up there. Bob and Francie had talked about one that they call Octopus Lake because of its many arms. The branch of the river that goes through the gorge apparently runs from it. The maps I have do not quite stretch that far and much of the country in that direction can only be guessed at.

North of the bluff on which I sat was a short bit of straggling bush, then a long slope up to an enticing, wavelike ridge, with other very walkable-looking peaks beyond. An area I can't wait to explore, but there is no time now.

A raven croaked and flapped onto a bleached pine snag, looking at me critically. But he didn't look clairvoyant this time, only hungry. The wind caught him, and he lifted off and sailed away.

I have been a painter for many years. With every good intention, I had art materials flown in on an early plane, but I could not summon up the energy while I worked on the cabin.

It was so long since I had attempted a painting, I was reluctant to put paint to paper. I had to make myself squeeze out the colours and start to push them around. But at once there was a small stir of excitement at the sight and texture of the medium as it began to relate to its space and its neighbouring marks.

Usually, when I am new to a place, my first attempts at painting are trite and frustrating; I wonder if I will ever be able to paint again. But, if I am there long enough, and if I am lucky, something suddenly happens. It is usually far removed from the images I had originally in my mind. This is the subject taking over and exerting its own influence and it is inexplicably wonderful when it occurs. Sometimes, for painting after painting, I can do nothing wrong. Spells like these are rare, but they are the nuggets that keep any artist prospecting away.

After such a long break from painting, I was expecting little, but after two or three scribbles, the magic began. I splattered paint with brush and fingers, threw colour about with abandon, and added jabs and smudges of pastel and charcoal. I actually liked what I was producing although I shall no doubt look back on them in the future with a certain amount of contempt; however, for the moment, I am excited by them. I think it was because I had become so involved with the place, so bound up in it, that it simply had to come out somehow. Not that my pictures were particularly recognizable as this mountain or that tree, but the feelings came out strongly. Three paintings, in fact, were self-portraits, something I have never tried before. Is it because I have been so much alone? One was done after a wind warning had been issued on the radio and part of my mind must have been waiting for it to pounce. When I looked in the mirror, I was conscious only of two eyes, a nose, and a mouth, and the way the snow-filtered light fell on them from the windows. To fill in a blank piece of paper, I indicated the hurricane lamp, which I could see in the mirror behind my head. Then I set it up and looked at what I had got. Although I had not been aware of drawing it, the face that stared back at me was full of apprehension; the shoulders were hunched, the green in the shadows was sickly. In fact, I never had a breath of wind, for it was a southeast storm and I have since learned that when the wind is that way, I have dead calm. But I did not know that then, and the anticipated storm is undeniably in the painting. I shall call it "Wind Warning." People will relate it to the hurricane lamp behind me, but that is just a coincidence.

November 18, 1988

There was a new, windless fall of snow. The lake in front of the cabin was not frozen and the flakes formed a curious grey sludge on top of the water, an intriguing tactile contrast to the pure white fluffballs on the black-walled rocks. A puff of wind and it all disintegrated. Soon the snow was coming down horizontally again, plastering rocks, trees, and the cabin with white on the windward side. There was enough to shovel around the bottoms of the cabin walls and it is amazing what a difference that has made to the temperature inside; I often need the door open when the stove is lit.

The snow is not particularly easy to walk through. It innocently hides all manner of holes and pitfalls and it is very slippery. It clogs the dog's toes and gets deep into her fur.

Behind Crescent Island, the ice is already two inches thick and I have walked on it with caution in places. Although the water seems to be shallow there, I would not like to fall in because not far below the surface is a soft, floating silt so deep that a canoe paddle thrust into it cannot touch the bottom. When the water was at its lowest and I could still canoe round there, the top layer of sludge was disturbed into milky clouds by the passage of the boat, releasing a barrage of hydrogen sulphide bubbles. Some of the sunrises I witnessed were distinctly smelly.

The ice spread far out up the lake and I thought it was going to stay, but as I write a sullen wind is gnawing at it. The new ice undulates. Long, dark cracks appear and disappear, and the edge is crumbling. Outside, the hiss and tinkle of the broken pieces are audible even above the threnody of the wind.

I leave tomorrow. It is the federal election on Tuesday and it will take me most of the three days to get to the polling station, for the alpine route is now too risky and, as there will be no ice strong enough to walk on, I will have to go via Banana Lake and take the longest and most uncomfortable ways to negotiate everything. One disadvantage of living here is that when I have outside commitments fairly close together, it is often not practical for me to come home between them, particularly when travelling conditions are so bad. So I shall have to stay out for a while. Two weeks after the election, I am to have an art show at Salmon Arm. I already have a store of paintings at Nimpo ready to go, but I will take the new work with me. They are wrapped in garbage bags inside an unused length of stove pipe. They should travel well enough that way, as long as I don't drop them in the river. After the show I will, I hope, have more money for supplies and will have to spend time shopping. I will be staying with friends for Christmas and for most of January I have been asked to house-sit. So at this stage I am not at all sure when I will be home.

The only time I have travelled the complete winter route was three years ago on the second visit I made to this place. The stretch as far as Sam's cabin is familiar enough and when I hiked down by Avalanche Lake, I travelled the section below its junction with my river to Rimarko. But there are still fifteen miles or so in the middle that will be virtually new to me. No doubt, as usual, there will be a dearth of blazes and a plethora of windfalls and swamps. Banana Lake will not be frozen and so I will have to find a way around it. A river crossing somewhere en route is unavoidable, not a pleasant prospect at this time of year. I shall carry an old pair of sneakers specifically for the river crossing so my boots stay dry; bare feet become numb too quickly in icy water and there is a real danger of damaging them on rocks if they are not protected.

Everything is ready for me to leave at the first glimmer of light in the morning. The cans are in the root cellar and all the rest of the food, even that from the kitchen shelves, is in the attic. The lamps are filled and, when I go, they will be placed on the floor, their chimneys in a box of socks, so that there is less risk of mess and

damage should something get in and knock them over. The shutters
are up and all the gas and kerosene is wired down in the old food
crate, which now makes a useful fuel store. It is some distance away
from the building and therefore a little unhandy, but a plus on the
safety side should there ever be a fire.

There have been no sign of bears for a long time, but when the
spawning is finished down in the Atnarko Valley, which will not be
long now, the bears will have to climb up high again to find snow
deep enough to den. I suppose that there is always a possibility one
could still pass by, looking for a bedtime snack.

Chapter 14

March 2, 1989

The windows of the cabin are covered with sweeping forests of ice ferns so thick that breathing on them cannot dissipate them. The small hole that I scratched with my fingernail a few minutes ago is already filmed and opaque. Beyond them, the lake is a dead slate blue and silent, the sky greenish and etherial, the mountains coldly orange in the pre-dawn glow. A half-inch of cocoa, left in a mug overnight on the windowsill, is frozen solid. Trees are popping and the house logs crack like pistol shots; the metal of the roof vibrates in sympathy. A thermometer tacked to a post on the porch reads -35°C.

But the night that I have just experienced, my first one at home since I left in November, was far more comfortable than the one before it. The trip back here was an experience I have no desire to repeat.

The journey started innocuously enough, in fact, the weather, as can often happen so close to the coast, was too warm, with temperatures above freezing.

Bob, Francie, and Patrick were at Rimarko. Trapping was finished, but a tent of theirs still stood at the mouth of the river; they were expecting a friend and were going to take him for a snow machine trip to the back of their line.

Francie had been listening to the weather forecast. She warned me that an arctic front was coming, but I was more relieved by the news than anything, because colder temperatures would mean better travelling conditions.

Charlotte Lake was well frozen with only a little slushy snow on top. I left Rimarko at noon and reached the tent (pitched on a low, log wall and equipped with a stove so it was quite comfortable inside) well before nightfall. During the night the temperature dropped perhaps fifteen degrees, which seemed perfect.

Now for my list of mistakes. I had thought that I could ski most of the way home, but I am not very good at it and found the skis sunk impossibly once off the ice. Even on the lake they had been far less practical than I had anticipated, for carrying a heavy pack both upset my balance and made my shoulders ache so fiercely that they were sore for the rest of the journey. I knew snowshoes would be necessary on the rougher parts of the trip, so I had brought them along, but it was obvious now that they would be the only footwear appropriate. I should have dumped the skis by the tent, left a note, and picked them up next time I was through, but I still had visions of effortless glides down sunny, frozen lakes at home during the remainder of the winter. So I strapped the skis to my pack, consequently snagging every branch within reach, usually, moreover, one that was more than ready to free itself from its weary accumulation of snow.

Secondly, I was wearing the wrong clothes. It was snowing a little when I left the tent. The previous time I had tramped through snow-covered brush, my clothes had become so wet from snow melt dumping off the branches I might just as well have been in the rain. So this time I wore rain gear. However, it trapped my body moisture against me and my clothes were soaked. Worse, I was wearing a cotton T-shirt, which is a disaster in subzero weather, for it keeps the body's moisture close to the skin and wicks in the cold.

Bob and Francie did not trap along my branch of Whitton Creek this year so there was no snowmobile trail to follow. (Their routes were too far out of my way to be practical.) So I broke my own trail all the way. The snow in the bush was soft and deep. I had expected to make better progress in the swamps, but there the under-snow was composed of billions of tiny, ice ball-bearings. I sank abysmally, even on snowshoes; often the only way to make progress was to scramble around the edges of the swamps among the trees. The snow was firmer under them, but even the animals had avoided making trails there, for the branches of the trees swept the ground. Every one that I snagged with those ridiculous skis dumped a new load of snow down my neck. I lost the trail more than I found it and floundered miserably in horrible tangles of windfalls. As the river was frozen over, I could not use its sound as a guide as I had done before. In places, had I known the country better, the river might have been safe enough to walk on, but much of it was humped over rocks and rapids with black glimpses of open water visible in deep holes and cracks. I deemed it not worth the risk.

About halfway along the river there are two small waterfalls; around them is the steepest part of the trail. I was very tired by this stage, but if I tried to rest for more than a few moments, I became so cold that I was in agony before I started again. The temperature was obviously still dropping fast. A gusty wind was roaring in the tree tops but luckily very little of it reached me. I was too cold to stop and make a fire. I ate a few dates, chewing them frozen. I could not help but think what a long way they had travelled from their origins. There was nothing to drink because all open water was in the middle of the river and I did not dare attempt the ice at the edges of the holes to fetch it. Eating unmelted snow is one of the surest ways to reduce body heat.

I am often asked, "How do you walk such a long way?" and I reply, "By putting one foot in front of the other." Which is perfectly true; but I cannot explain to them that sometimes it is because it is impossible to stop. Barbie wrote me a poem for Christmas. She presented it to me as I came through Rimarko and I carried it folded in my shirt pocket. It begins: "You make it look so easy, striding down the trail, long arms swinging." But in times like these the body screams in the kind of protest few people will ever experience; the muscles have to be coerced into performing beyond fatigue and beyond pain. But it is amazing how much can be demanded of frail human tissue when it is necessary. It was not the first time that I have felt that I could not move another step, and yet, somehow, I always keep going. No, Barbie, it is not always easy, we each of us have a price to pay no matter which way we choose to live.

As I finally stepped onto Banana Lake, the wind hit me. It was at my back, otherwise I might have been in serious trouble. I had expected the snow on the lake to be firmer, but it was knee deep and loose on the top and the snowshoes sank most of the way to the ice. Twenty agonized steps and a rest. Twenty steps and a rest. The lake is four miles long. I clung to the west side, hoping for a little protection from the wind, but whirling dervishes of snow came flying up the lake, pounding me like a punching bag. Twenty steps and a rest. I was truly frightened now. I understood very little about hypothermia but was well aware that the mind can become affected and I might no longer be thinking coherently. Twenty steps and a rest. The dog plodded in misery behind.

Sam's cabin seemed a lifetime away, but I reached it sometime after dark. I could just make out the way in the pale gloom of the snow. I flung off my pack. Stumbled round to the ladder and climbed the steep roof to take the pots off the stove pipe. Groped in the dim interior for the shavings and kindling I'd left handy. Reached in an inner pocket for matches.

And that, I thought, was the end of me. I could not make my fingers hold the match. They did not seem particularly cold, but it required enormous concentration to make my left hand squeeze my right hand with enough force to clasp the match to strike it. It lit first try. How precious was that tiny flame. The shavings caught, and then the kindling. It was then, and only then, that I started to shiver. I shook and shuddered uncontrollably. My clothes steamed.

The cabin meant survival, but it was a far from comfortable night. Because the trappers had not been this way this year, there was not much firewood and I used what there was sparingly. The stove was on a platform of rocks to keep it from the wood-chip floor where I lay in my sleeping bag, and all its meagre heat fled upwards, missing me entirely. Absent chinking and the damage the bear had done had created massive holes in the walls; draughts whistled through them to feed the fire. If I opened my eyes in the dark, the fluid that covered them became stiff and gluey as if it was freezing. The neck of my sleeping bag absorbed the moisture from my breath and soon froze into a band of iron. I have never been so cold, nor had such a long night, in my life.

Grey fingers of dawn illuminated the cracks between the chinkless logs and day had finally arrived. The morning was windless and, once the mountain shadow had retreated far enough, brilliantly sunny. With only half a day's travel to go, I could afford to wait until the temperature had climbed a little, which it can do quite dramatically on a sunny day. I started hiking wearing everything I possessed — and was instantly far too hot and had to spend time stuffing half my clothes back into the pack.

My little cabin looked suprisingly normal after all I'd been

through. Nothing was disturbed except an almost full toilet roll I had inadvertently left on the kitchen bench, and which had been chewed into little bits. Fine powdery snow had drifted in around the door; where it lay on the floor it was laced with a delicate tracery of mouse tracks.

There must have been around four feet of snow on the ground around the cabin, but Nuk Tessli had blown the porch fairly clear. He had also stripped most of the foundations of their banked insulation. So while the stove was roaring and a pail of snow was melting on the top, I shovelled snow round the bottoms of the walls once more. It was afternoon by that time and the sun shone through the cabin windows at full strength, but neither it nor the roaring stove could melt the thick layer of frost on the glass.

Within an hour of my arrival, a mess of cornbeef hash and tea were ready. I grabbed a knife and fork — and dropped them because they bit. Despite being stored close to the stove, they were still so cold that they frost-burned my fingers. It would take a couple of days to warm the cabin through properly. I picked up the knife and fork in a pot holder and tossed them onto the stove top to warm up.

Now the sun is high and the shining winter world is beckoning. There is nothing fearsome about it now that I have a good shelter to return to. I have a new camera and I want to take some pictures of the cabin before it warms up and the snow slides off the roof.

CHAPTER 15

March 4, 1989

It is much warmer; -15°C first thing this morning. The layer of ice on the windows vanished quite quickly after I had lit the stove. The radio came through and the forecast is for Pacific storms by tomorrow, "bringing," the weatherman says, "southwest winds and the warm weather we've all been waiting for."

Richard keeps a Cessna 180 on skis at the hangar in Anahim Lake during the winter. They are the kind of skis that are levered under the wheels after the plane has taken off from an ordinary runway. Richard was away, and a man called Floyd Vaughn brought in my supplies.

I have known Floyd for many years, because he used to fly my equipment down to Lonesome Lake, the nearest place to the Atnarko cabin at which he could land.

Floyd had never landed at my lake before, but he knew it well enough, and swooped down onto the ice well beyond the islands and their attendant ring of rocks. By the time I had snowshoed out to him, he was firing stuff onto the snow; it was still very cold, for it was the day after I had arrived, and I had brought a sleeping bag out to the plane with me, in which to wrap the box of vegetables so that they would not freeze.

Floyd has to be the least talkative person I have ever met. His silences are not uncomfortable, he simply seems to have nothing he feels obliged to say; nonetheless, he suprised me by acquiescing when I invited him in for coffee. I suppose he was curious to see what the cabin looked like. I strapped the vegetables to my pack frame and he picked up a couple of fuel cans and shuffled through the snow behind me. And thus Floyd became the second human being to enter my door.

Most people in this country have had some cabin-building experience. Floyd's only comment was that some of the logs were mightily twisted. The sun was not yet far enough round to shine in at the windows and, after the brilliance of the morning outside, the cabin looked rough and drab with its naked fibreglass chinking and temporary, log-round furniture.

Floyd was soon looking at his watch. He could not leave the plane too long as the motor would start to cool. He told me that the temperature had reached -42°C on the night I spent at Sam's cabin.

In the dazzling, blue-etched world, the red Cessna glowed like a firebird. The Pacific wind was starting and long plumes of snow were flying from the summits of the mountains. The plane's propellors whipped chunks of snow from the lake into the air and cut them into

fragments. As the plane turned, its blizzard engulfed me. Needles of ice penetrated my hair and I hung onto a box that was in danger of blowing away. The angle of the blast changed as the plane headed into the wind, its motors roared, then suddenly it was skimming over the surface and soaring into the air. It banked, flashing carmine wings against the sun, and was gone. The rising wind hissed snow skeins across the surface of the lake.

To pack the equivalent amount of gear the two miles from Lonesome Lake to the Atnarko cabin would have taken a week. This took perhaps an hour, but it did not mean that I enjoyed tramping back and forth with all the loads. I wonder how many miles I have walked on this place, simply carrying things?

The bulk of this plane load is the first installment of the all-too-numerous possessions that have been cluttering friends' sheds and basements for the last while. It was like Christmas all over again; the contents of some of the packages I have not seen for years.

How homey the place suddenly looked that night, with the books on the shelf; the woven blanket (and sheets, at last, as opposed to a sleeping bag) on the bed; the two new kerosene lamps with their clean, white flames; and a large Emily Carr calendar, a Christmas present, hanging on the wall. I wish Floyd could have seen it like this.

A feast of carrots, onions, and potatoes for supper, plus the great treat of fresh meat. Roger Folsom at the Wilderness Rim Resort shot a moose in the fall, and he and Gloria have sent some of it in on the plane. The other half a dozen packages are still frozen and I have put them in a bucket and buried them in a snowdrift. Lonesome, fortunately, is a reliable dog where food is concerned.

The vegetables and eggs, which must be neither frozen nor kept too warm, are the most difficult things to store at this time of year. During cold spells, they must be lifted onto a table; when the stove is lit during the day, they have to be moved back down again. I rarely keep the fire going at night, because I find it too hot to sleep.

March 6, 1989

The skis that I packed home with such laborious effort have proved to be useless. In fact, ice travel this year is more difficult than in the bush, where the force of snow, dumping off the trees, has compacted the surface a little more. But even there I still sink considerably and it is going to be hard work to move very far for quite a while. I need snowshoes as soon as I step off the porch, even to go to the outhouse.

When I visited with Bob and Francie at Rimarko on my way in, Bob taught me something about snowshoe bindings. The standard commercial ones with buckles all over them might be impossible to reach and undo if you go through the ice. Bob uses a length of rope attached to the toe piece and twisted round the foot in a figure-of-eight pattern.

I have a bunch of spare backpack straps so used them instead of a length of rope. The bindings can be kicked off without having to bend down; they seem to work very well.

Bob told me he goes through the ice to some degree or other quite often. Two years ago he lost a snow machine in thirty feet of water on Avalanche Lake. Francie was behind on another machine with Patrick, who would then be six. As soon as she saw steam (from Bob's exhaust pipe as it hit the water) she veered to shore. Bob was unable to pull himself onto the ice, and Francie had to cut a long pole to fish him out.

By Skidoo, they were only a couple of hours away from Rimarko, where they returned as soon as Bob had been thawed and dried out by a large fire. A few days later, the temperature dropped and the lake froze again. By cutting a hole through the new ice, they could see the snow machine sitting on the bottom. With a grappling hook, they snagged the snow machine. It was not hard to pull it to the surface, but extracting it from the embrace of the water was not something Bob wants to do every day of his life.

The water had done very little damage; the motor had to be dried out but it started without a lot of trouble. Patrick's sleeping bag was wet but the flour had absorbed water only on the outside, forming an impermeable crust, thus protecting the bulk of it. The scope on the rifle fared the worst. As it hit the subzero air, the water inside froze instantly, expanded, and broke it.

The promised Pacific front arrived. At first fine snow blew in on the wind and scratched against the window panes. Then the temperature rose above freezing, +5°C by my thermometer. The snow immediately became sticky and soggy and horrible to travel on. The accumulation on my roof fell with a horrendous crash and I heard, quite complacently at first, a muffled regular rhythm of drips — until I realized that the drips were inside the house, up in the attic.

Snow had blown up the sloping metal and penetrated the gaps between it and the ridge cap. When I erected it I thought it peculiar that the ridge cap was smooth when the roofing sheets were ridged — I could not see how the joint could possibly be weatherproof. The snow is on a bit of flat ceiling that lies on horizontal braces near the top of the rafters. It was nailed in place before the roof was put on and there is no way I can get at it now. So the snow will have to stay until it drips itself away. I knew I had been saving all my empty tin cans for something. I have been up on the roof (thanks to the deep snow piles under the eaves, the ladder can now reach the top with ease) and tried to block the gap with roof tar. But the brown metal warmed so much in the sun it caused the tar to melt and dribble down the roof and away from the holes. Not only do I still have gaps, but I now have a mess as well.

March 7, 1989

About halfway through the morning, I heard a snow machine. It had to be either Bob or Francie, for no one else is ever in this country in the winter — it is much too daunting for recreational travellers.

It was Francie with Patrick travelling behind her on skis, joined to the snow machine by a long piece of rope. Bob was out with his friend, picking up unused food from the caches, for they did not want to leave anything for the problem bear.

Francie and Patrick arrived in a squall, completely whitened on one side by the wet snow. It cracked like an eggshell as they shook themselves free of it. "Good god!" said Francie, commenting on the wind as she wrestled with the door and dived thankfully off the streaming porch. "That's nothing," I replied. "You should see it when its really blowing." Why, the cabin wasn't even shaking.

Francie has done her fair share of cabin building and she wasn't about to say, "Fancy, you did this all on your own; how wonderful. Especially for a woman!" In fact, now that I am here and Barbie and Alex are at Rimarko, the "weaker sex" has somewhat overtaken the country.

My cabin would not have suited Francie. There were too many

windows for her — that meant too much firewood to haul to keep it warm. And the wind and horizontal snow beating against the west windows were not making a very good impression. But the cabins Francie inhabits — the one at Rimarko; a summer one at Anahim for when they are not on the trail, and, on occasions, Sam Sulin's cabin — are wanted only for shelter. Her material desires are far fewer than mine.

It was wonderful to have visitors but they did not stay long. Bob would set off to look for them if they did not get back to camp within a certain time. The snow still lashed at the cabin — this time they would have it in their faces. I stood at the window and watched them, two dark, bowed figures bent over the snow machine. Francie's arm jerked a time or two as she pulled the starter, then the snow machine drew away, the bent dot of Patrick, who insisted that he did not want to ride behind the windshield, at the end of his tow rope. The lake was a featureless void in the blowing snow. Slowly, slowly, the figures were swallowed by the storm.

Had they waited another hour, the snow would have stopped. The sun even shone a little. Odd swirls of wind whipped the snow into spirals which danced and jerked like puppets across the lake. I slid my feet into the snowshoes and plodded out into it, following a route through the forest that I had made the day before. There was not a sign of my tracks in the open places and very little even in the shelter of the trees. On the lake, the wind had sculpted fascinating patterns on the surface of the snow and on land it had rebuilt and refined the drifts, putting a sharper, knife-edge crease onto them.

CHAPTER 16

March 16, 1989

By breaking trail as far as I am able one day then capitalizing on it the next, I am gradually extending my knowledge of the country and linking together the bumps and hollows I can see around me with the larger features delineated on the map. It is wonderfully exciting to tread on new territory; there is always that delicious thrill of never knowing what is going to be around the next corner.

The little creek not far north of me was my first target. It took me two attempts to reach the first of the lakes, for the creek had all but disappeared under a whipped-cream blanket of snow and could not be distinguished from a number of other gullies and hollows, so at first I lost it. In the tiny meadows, it had carved strange abstract swirls in the snow, and where it had been steep and noisy in the fall, it could still just be heard, gurgling hollowly somewhere far beneath my feet. I fell into it once. It was enormously difficult to extricate myself for, when I pushed with my arms, they simply sank. I writhed for a while like a beetle on its back. But off came the snowshoe as it was designed to do and I was able to roll over and put my weight on the still-shod foot. The misplaced snowshoe had touched the water and the air temperature was cold enough to freeze snow onto it instantly. It must have weighed several pounds and was impossible to clean off. I could not walk without it and my progress home was with a laborious dot-and-carry motion as I heaved the monster snowshoe forward at every step. I was a lot more careful with the creek after that.

The second lake was perhaps a mile beyond the first. How enchanting it is to emerge onto a new shore. Had anyone every stood there before me? Bob Cohen probably had, although it must be many years since he came this way; and perhaps Sam Sulin. But that might well be all. What a precious untouched inheritance they have left me; how carefully I must treat it to pass it on unmarred.

Along the creek and round the edges of the lake was an otter track. Presumably there was fish for him in the water, or else he would not be there. But it was hard to imagine what he lived on. How far can he go under the ice before he has to turn back? Does he ever make mistakes? The distinctive track, a deep, routed trough deep-pricked at regular intervals by the animal's feet, emerged from holes in the snow above the creek, wound around the bumps and hollows for a while, then dived out of sight again where the otter must have travelled along the creek bed. On the lakes he seemed to travel with a run — slide — run — slide motion; downslopes were accomplished in one, long glissade: the original cross-country skier.

Other tracks on the snow are rare, except for those of mice and squirrels and neat pairs of dots at large intervals which must belong to weasels. Occasionally I stumble upon those of a ptarmigan or hare or fox, but I never see the animals, nor any sign of deer or moose or wolf. They have all gone further down where the snow is not as deep. Once blurred, round tracks of an unfamiliar interval trotted across the snow and I think this was a lynx. There must be marten, too, for that is what Bob and Francie trap. Marten eat squirrels, which are plentiful and obvious, but the predators themselves are very secretive, leaving few signs of their passage. They must either keep to the trees or follow the squirrels under the snow.

Having established the route along Otter Creek (it would seem as appropriate a name as any) I next crossed it and fought my way to the top of the lookout bluff. In the fall, the ascent had not been difficult, but on snowshoes it was ludicrous. I slipped and slithered, lost snowshoes, clung to trees, and made use of every minute deformity of the land to gain height. Poor Lonesome struggled along in my wake. Francie told me that usually the snow has glazed by now; she and Bob were suprised to find how soft it still is.

The wind had filled the hollows between the great boulders below the bluff itself, but at the western end, the rocks had been blown
clear. I clutched the snowshoes under my arm to climb the rocks,
then tramped across the unmarked top to the viewpoint.

There was my world laid out beneath me as before, but now
almost a stranger in its winter coat. My lake was an unblemished
sheet of white, except for a tiny line of snowshoe tracks around its
edge. The trail was clearer as it wandered round Otter Lake, and
sharp and distinct on the broad, wind-smoothed highway below the
bluff. Why is it so difficult to walk in a straight line on a flat surface?
The tracks lurched and wavered like those of a drunk.

The sky was blue and clear to the east, the mountains bright and
cleanly shadowed. But cloud was spreading rapidly from the west in
long, streaming mare's tails. Even as I sat there, the cloud swallowed
the sun and it went out like a light. Another Pacific front coming in.

One day, I climbed as far as the bluff, then continued along the
broken ground to the ridge beyond, which has beckoned me for so
long. The climb was gradual and seemed marvellously open, but
what was beneath me? Swamp? Rock? Balsam fir? Would it be the
kind of footing I could expect tourists to cope with? It was heavy
going in the snowshoes, but the day was glorious, sharp and cool
and very clear. I rounded the shoulder of the mountain and reached
the tree line at about the same time. The bluff looked small and far
away, and more peaks had emerged all around the horizon. I was a
little above, and could see into the pass that Bob and Francie and
company must have used to go out, but there was no trace of them
there. It is a long pass, with, according to the map, several small
lakes hidden beneath the smooth whiteness; on foot it would be a
long way before reaching the shelter of the trees at the far side. Bob
tells me that it is imperative to find the exact spot for dropping off
the pass, otherwise you land either in a bad canyon or a terrible mess
of windfall. The land drops fairly steeply and the valley, yet another
branch of Whitton Creek, arrives eventually back at Charlotte Lake.
It would be fun to go out that way sometime, but I would want to
be very sure of the weather.

The sun, as I stood on the rim of North Pass, was blinding, and
the sky a springlike blue. It is spring not too far away from here. The
snow will be going from Nimpo and the drab, grey ground will be
showing. Down in Bella Coola, the aromatic cottonwood buds will
be fattening and ready to burst. Even here, a few spring birds are

beginning to trickle through: juncos; mountain chickadees; pine grosbeaks; and nuthatches with their reedy little calls. Downy wood-peckers whistle and peck at trees with a sharp, rhythmic tapping.

March 21, 1989

The equinox. (I think: I am never quite sure if it is the 21st or 22nd.)

It is another gorgeous day, frost in the morning, everything crisp, fresh, and dazzling with the afternoon sun suggesting T-shirt weather.

The chimney has not been drawing well, so I dragged the ladder around so that I could climb up and sweep it. Rods that screw to-gether to push a chimney brush are ridiculously expensive so I tied my brush securely to a rope fashioned of recycled bale string (friends who have a ranch save it for me — where would I be without this wonderful material?) and shoved it down the chimney with my ski poles tied together at the ends. This arrangement took the soot down as far as the elbow joint in the main room and, by taking the elbow apart carefully, I could get most of the soot outside intact. A bath was, needless to say, the next priority.

The washtub full of melting snow has been almost constantly on the stove, but I wonder if I'm getting enough minerals from the water — domestic sheep can suffer if they have nothing but snow to drink for too long (mind you, I do not reckon to be producing lambs in the spring). Still, I thought it time to cut a waterhole in the lake.

The spot in front of the cabin where water is collected in the summer would not be a good choice at this time of year because there it is shallow and full of rocks and I would have no idea what I was going to hit with the chain saw. But a step away from the wharf logs on the other side of the point I know the lake to be at least six feet deep and unobstructed. I put the long, lumber-making bar on the bigger saw and lugged it and the shovel and the pry-bar onto the lake. There were two feet of snow to shovel away, most of it the tiny round ice balls — no wonder I sank so easily into it. The Inuit have, apparently, some thirty words for snow in their language, but I would think even they would not be enough to describe the incredible number of textures so close to the coast. Air humidity must be an important factor, for temperatures of -20°C will produce very dif-ferent snow in Bella Coola from that which falls here.

The long bar on the chain saw was superfluous, for in about six inches, great gouts of water fountained up with the whirling chain. Not far below was another layer of ice; the water was either trapped overflow, or a spring from the nearby shore. The lower layer of ice will be a great advantage for if anything is inadvertently dropped into the hole, it will not sink out of sight. The water is a little brownish and a few fir needles are floating in it, but that won't hurt. I have no worries about the water here: I don't have the giardia that is spreading into areas with more human use.

I was curious about the depth of ice further out into the lake where it was solid. It took two tries to reach the water, for the twenty-six-inch bar on the saw was not long enough to penetrate at the first go; there were about thirty inches of ice in all. Roger Folsom at Wilderness Rim had given me a few tips about ice-cutting. For a water or fishing hole, it is better to make the sides slanting so that the bottom of the hole is narrower than the top; thus the block can easily be levered out.

Roger runs his saw dry of oil by cutting firewood with it for a while. Despite falling and bucking two dead trees near the cabin, the chain on my saw was still not clean and until I have scooped out the residue of oil on the water I will not be able to use my new over-flow well.

I had planned on using the winter falling trees and making more lumber, even skidding logs over the ice. But the loose snow made it impossible — it was far too nerve-wracking to cut down anything but the easiest and most necessary trees while wearing snowshoes. The path that I have beaten to the outhouse now supports me in the mornings even without those encumbrances, but immediately I step off it, I sink to my waist. The firewood trees were small and leaning, but even so, I did not like falling them when I could not jump quickly out of the way. They will provide me with just enough fuel until I go out as long as it doesn't get really cold again, which seems unlikely now. I never found the woodpile that I left behind the cabin. It is close to a particular tree which I know I have not mistaken, but I have dug and dug without result. There must be a big drift there. The snow depth has not lessened a whit despite the warmer weather. The tip of a stick just outside the kitchen window was level with the snow when I first arrived; it was covered for a while and now it is just peeping through again. It is a little eerie to remember that every-where I go I'm walking about four feet off the ground.

I had great plans for all the art work that I was going to do as well, but that elusive flame of creativity that erupted in the fall seems to have vanished. The paint is dead, the spark is gone. Why is it so hard to grasp? What makes the pattern of lines and shapes so right one time and a total failure the next? Why can't I do something with the orange light of the setting sun when it bronzes the twisted trees along the shoreline and sends elongated purple shadows along the lake? When my own shadow becomes a monster with a teeny head and massive triangular legs shod in great webbed boats that lift and fall in rhythm? And then the light is gone and the snow is suddenly luminous and coolly blue. There is the immediate nip of falling temperature, the increased awareness of sound: the scrape and flop of snowshoes, the creak of the cabin door, the rattle of the stove. Yellow light springs from the lamps and, out on the lake, the last, frost-green glow fades in the sky.

Why can't I do something with that?

March 23, 1989

In the earth, there are several species of an extremely common creature called a springtail. They are part of the fauna that decompose organic matter in the soil. They are visible to the naked eye, but most are unnoticed except one species which emerges on the surface of the snow en masse. They look like the dumped contents of a can of ground black pepper, from which individuals leap high into the air, earning them the name of "snowflea." They do this by means of a hook under their abdomen which grasps, then releases their tail. Richard Perry in *Mountain Wildlife* says that the hook is the strongest material yet known on this earth.

Presumably it is the mating urge that drives them through four feet of snow, a considerable journey if you are only the size of a pepper grain. Nature has certainly devised some peculiar obstacle races for the procreation of her species. The springtails come up only when it is warm and are visible for only a few days in the year — but not the same ones every year. Obviously, then, it is temperature rather than daylight length that is the stimulating factor, but surely the soil cannot be much warmer yet. Do the insects lie just below the surface of the snow and wait for their grand entrance into the world? I have carefully separated shovelfuls of snow but I cannot see a trace of them if they are not visible on the top.

The Clark's nutcracker is a common bird that lives here year round. At first glance it resembles a whiskeyjack, for it is also a grey jay, but the nutcracker's beak is long and swordlike and it has a very different call. Whiskeyjacks have a large repertoire of sound, most of it very melodious, but all the nutcrackers seem to do is screech. And what a screech! It has to be one of the most jarring calls to human ears. But no doubt the nutcrackers find it pleasing. A pair are building in a lodgepole that leans over the edge of the lake. It is touching to watch them, for they arrange and rearrange what to me is a loose muddle of sticks with great care and tenderness. Each bird waits until its partner has finished before flying in with its own offering; the assiduously collected twigs seem to be positioned with the same triumphant sense of achievement that I had with my logs. And as they work, is it possible that there is a different tone to their screeching? Are these ear-grating squawks a little softer and more mellow? Are they a declaration of love?

When I was in the Arctic, my camera failed me and, in an effort to record the wonder and diversity of the wild flowers, I started to draw them. They were just little pen sketches touched with watercolour, but the occupation quickly turned into something of a passion. I also found I learned a huge amount. Details that I had never properly observed, like the number of petals and reproductive parts, how the leaves were joined to the stalk, and whether they were hairy or toothed, were easily cemented in my mind; taxonomy at once became clear.

My great ambition is to explore every part of the country around me and record the growing things. Apart from a few very brief expeditions, none of the central Coast Range has been studied. The field guides that are available have been written for other, more accessible areas; for instance, a good book on the Rockies, containing references for many hundreds of species, identifies perhaps fifty plants local to here. A book on the Yukon contributes a couple of dozen more. I like to think that in time I will become the expert of the area, even if it is by dint of there being no one else. Bob and Francie know where all manner of plants are growing but their taxonomy is shaky and their nomenclature somewhat individual.

The only plants available for recording at the moment are things that stick above the snow. Their intriguing details were apparent as soon as I took pen in hand: the minute patterns that discarded needles leave on twigs; the way the buds and cones are constructed. Before my new-found vision, I had often noticed in a vague sort of way that the tips of some of the spruce branches were dead. These were now revealed, not as a bunch of needles, but curious structures, conelike and hollow. The most interesting thing about them was that there were two types. Were they caused by an insect? Was one kind of these spiny chalices the result of an infected leaf bud and the other from a flower? Was it another kind of insect that deformed the ends of willow twigs and formed whorls of leaves that did not drop off but turned into perfect wooden roses? Then there was the mistletoe. To me, mistletoe conjures up the image of the broad-leaved evergreen (usually now made of plastic) associated with druids and kissing at Christmas, but this plant is only an inch or two long, yellow and leafless, and looks more like a fungus. It lives on lodgepoles; the affected branches swell disproportionately, like Popeye's arms: the twigs below the infection are stunted into "witches brooms" and they grow small, sickly looking needles. I now realize that the mistletoe has contributed as much to the bonsai distortions of the forest that surrounds me as the wind. A forester would no doubt tear his hair to look at it, but I am not programmed into an economic learning pattern and I find it beautiful.

There was a full moon last night. I paid homage to it by walking onto the lake. Wind had obliterated all previous tracks and I walked in the luminous darkness as if I was first arrival in an untrodden world. When I turned and looked behind me, I found that the round, twin lines of deep-cut prints had absorbed the moonlight strangely; apart from the moon itself, they were the brightest things to be seen. They looked etherial, as if they were made of phosphorescence, like a ship's wake, and would dissolve in an instant.

Alien paws.

Sasquatch prints.

CHAPTER 17

March 29, 1989

I took my sketchbook with me when I snowshoed up to Bob and Francie's pass again (I'll call it the North Pass). But the black scribbles on the cheap five-by-eight-inch sheets of paper could convey nothing of what I saw about me. I left in the frost and strong purple shadows of the early morning. Just beyond Ravens Bluff was a little hollow; the small trees that dotted it were covered, on their east sides only, with masses of two-inch crystals of ice. They looked like silver-feathered birds, crouching and quivering their plumes behind them in some exotic ritual. There was not a trace of hoar frost anywhere else. Some stray exhalation of warm air must have made its way into the hollow, but why it should have been there alone was a mystery.

I made such good time to the lookout point above the North Pass that the snow was still cool and firm and cried out for further travel. Should I drop into the pass and try to pick up the trapper's trail back to Cohen Lake? I should probably run into it if I cast about in the forest. I was standing at the west end of the North Ridge; from there it swelled into a bump a thousand feet higher that I thought I could climb. In summer I would not have hesitated, but it is always a little worrying to go very far beyond the shelter of the forest in winter. There was a milky haze behind the Coast Range, but otherwise not a cloud in the sky.

The route to the spine of the ridge was the steepest. The long, stitched line of my snowshoe tracks unwound behind me. The last few paces were so wind blown and icy that I took the snowshoes off and used their tails to batter steps. But from then on, the spine itself sloped gently. It had been so exposed to winds that in places the snow was packed as hard as concrete; in others it had been swept completely away. For the first time since I'd last left Rimarko Ranch, I could walk without snowshoes. How wonderful it was to shed those clumsy shackles. The dog, too, was ecstatic for she could run and roll without sinking; she trotted jauntily ahead, her tail waving.

But how slowly I climbed. One would think that with all these years of mountain travel my lungs would no longer labour, nor my legs ache. It seems ridiculous that such physical torture could result in pleasure. But in the mountains, when the ground lifts, the spirit soars. What is it about the land swooping away that excites the human emotion, that makes one feel like a king? No wonder Satan took his victims to the top of a mountain to tempt them.

In places a few small brown and scrubby plants were exposed. Would these brittle sticks ever come to life? How could they survive the tremendous wind chill on these bare ridges? A fox had travelled up here at some time. The small compressions of her dainty feet had defied the wind and they stuck out of the snow, a little row of buttons. What had she come up here for? Mice? Rabbits? Ptarmigan? I saw no other tracks. Once a flock of gusting brown birds bobbed and twittered over the ridge; I could not identify them.

The ridge culminated in one of those hummocky summits where it is difficult to decide which is the highest point. The view was magnificent. To the east, the rest of the North Ridge curved behind like a breaking wave. To the west was the pass that Bob and Francie had used and, behind it, a large and impressive section of the Coast Range. The two-thousand-foot drop to the pass was almost sheer. I felt perched and precarious, indefatigable now that I had stopped climbing. "I am the thousand winds that blow. I am the diamond glints of snow." Who needs wings to fly?

My lake was spread to the south, the forested hills and hollows behind it filled with the countless white splashes of more frozen lakes, while beyond them were the jagged blue teeth of the Waddington Range, perhaps sixty miles away. Mt. Waddington was first called

"Mystery Mountain," for its enticing summit could be seen only from the open sea. It took the Mundys, who were fascinated by it, several expeditions to find it, let alone climb it. People fly in by helicopter now.

From my perch on the ridge, I could see large sections of my snowshoe trail, winding down, smaller and smaller towards my lake. I could even see them among the islands around the point that housed the cabin, although the building itself was invisible. The trail was a coiled thread to which, like a shadow, I was inextricably attached; an umbilical cord that joined me to the hub of the wheel of my world.

I stayed for a long time on the ridge, trying to fix the images of sun and snow and emptiness in my mind. All too soon I must leave and travel through the stink and roar of roads and cities and endure the dreary monotony of having to make some money.

A high-altitude jet carved a brief white streak that furred and spread across the sky. What a strange world we live in where a handful of air-breathing creatures, encapsulated with their life-support systems, can be flung so casually through the heavens. What were those people thinking of up there? The movie? The next cup of coffee? Who would meet them at the airport? What would they see if they looked down to the wrinkled skin of the earth? A tree-farm licence? An adventure playground? A useless tract of rock and ice? Could the thought ever enter their heads, that, for a few brief seconds, they were the closest neighbours to a wilderness dweller?

April 1, 1989

The sun is a few minutes from oblivion. It has been shining all day, despite the heavy clouds hovering behind the mountains. It will be raining on the other side of the divide, but here a stiff southwest wind has shredded the clouds and whirled them across the sky.

I have realized that, if I leave on the day I originally planned, and if I take three days to reach Nimpo as is likely, I will arrive at Williams Lake at a weekend. Which means the banks will be closed and I will not be able to extract money from them. So I will have to leave a day earlier. I will have to ask about one of those cards you can use outside banking hours.

The bindings I made for my snowshoes have lasted well but the webbing has now disintegrated. Plastic bale string will have to fill the gaps. It is comparatively heavy and, when it frays, the snow balls up on it; but it is all I have and better than nothing. Rawhide is not the most practical stuff either for it is very heavy and breaks easily when it is wet.

Radio reception has been very poor for weeks. This is partly because the way sunrise and the clock time are presently related means that the CBC no longer broadcasts before daylight in the morning, which is the best time for receiving the signal. But also, the northern lights are very active and although they have not been very showy, they play havoc with reception. However, I picked up part of a broadcast and it seems that the forecast is uncertain; I can expect a mixed bag on my trip out.

I will be going tree-planting and will not be back here until June. The snow will have vanished, the lake will be open, and there will be bugs and bears to think about again. Before I leave, my food will go up into the attic (except for the remaining cans and potatoes) and the gas and kerosene must be taken to the fuel store. The wind drove the snow right between the logs of the crate and the whole store was totally packed with it; the fuel that I needed had to be dug out piecemeal. I shall also tack screening up around the windows that open before I leave. It looks horrible against the snow, but I've no doubt I shall be glad of it in June.

April 5, 1989

The dark has the amorphous quality of falling snow. It is a pale dark, for the moon rides somewhere above the overcast, and the sky between the trees and the abrupt white line of the mounded drifts in front of them are easily distinguished. But there is an absence of those minute details that are usually present even on the darkest nights, and there is a blankness to the filtered moonlight. I cannot see the falling flakes, but when I stumble along the beaten path on my morning pilgrimage to the outhouse, my skin still shrinking against the chill of clothes uninhabited through the cooling hours of the night, the snow has a new, muffled sound beneath my feet and my face is tickled with touches as delicate as kitten paws. As I trudge back inside and bend to adjust the stove, spangles of lamp-lit droplets tumble from my hair. The melting flakes on my shoulders wink briefly, defiant miniscule flashes which say "I exist," before vanishing forever.

I had thought of attempting the North Pass route, but the fresh snow has stopped me and I will travel via Banana Lake as usual. I am going only as far as Sam's cabin tonight, so don't need to leave too early.

It is a pretty picture that I will take with me to the outside world. It is daylight now, and the sun is shining through the falling snow. The mountains are emerging dreamily in the softly veiled light. Fresh caps of snow are piled on each bunch of needles on the graceful white-bark pines outside the window. Snowshoe gumbo before long, though, I fear.

It is warm in the cabin and the door is open. I can hear the reedy wheeze of a nuthatch and the faint burbling of the swelling river as it tumbles into the rapids below the outlet. I wonder what the crossings will be like? And the snow? Will I see bare ground at Charlotte Lake? And silver birch catkins and the emerald mist of unfolding leaves as I drive south along the highways?

I shall be like D.G. Jones:

" ... we shall walk
Somehow into summer."

Part Two

CHAPTER 18

June 29, 1989

I wait for a plane. It is a dull, cold morning, calm down here, but a strong southeast wind is dragging clouds halfway down the mountains between here and Nimpo that could well stop anyone flying this way. The forest is greeny grey and soft with rain; the lake leaden and wrinkled; the cabin suddenly tall and leggy after the snowbound image I took away with me; the debris of messy, brown-needled brushpiles and yellow sawdust ugly on the ground.

But it is wonderful to be home at last. The quiet; the freedom of thought: it is only here that my mind can range unfettered. Only here that other things don't constantly pick away at its edges.

I had a fairly predictable trip out to the road in April. There was only one incident of note. The crossing below Sam's cabin was smooth and white, but there were open holes in the river close by. I shuffled over with some trepidation, but safely enough. A few minutes later, once the cap was off the stovepipe and the fire was lit, I came back down to the river to fetch a pail of water. As my snowshoes clattered

on the edge of the ice, there was a great crack and a soft woosh —
the whole centre of the river subsided.

Mindful of the previous summer's bear at Sam's cabin, and the
way he had been foiled by the skimpy bit of wire on the door, I
wired the door in three different places before I left. I also pounded
hefty bolts of wood across the window holes, using the loose-headed
axe and spikes I found in a can.

I spent two months tree-planting, an occupation that has been my
main source of income for the last few years. I have a love-hate relationship with this job — I like working outdoors; cutblocks apart,
the country is often magnificent; some of the people are fascinating;
and of course I love the money. But most of the time I am miserable,
particularly when the weather is bad. The ugliness of the aftermath
of logging, the cut-throat fighting for the last dollar, and the constant proximity of fifty other people jammed elbow to elbow, all take
their toll. One day, some bigwigs from the logging company (which
happened to be Weyerhauser) visited us. It was hot; the block was
burned and looked like pictures of wartime trenches; black ash coated
our filthy clothes and bit into our lungs; pickups and the refrigerator unit to keep the trees cool roared; and a dozen of us were fighting for
the last tree spaces. The collar-and-tie official, wearing an orange hard
hat (although there was no vegetation higher than six inches as far as
the eye could see) happened to pick on me to speak to. "And how,"
he said benignantly, "are you enjoying your wilderness experience?"

How wonderful it was to head north again, all my problems
dropping away with the miles. (Not quite all, for my truck had a
badly leaking transfer case which all sorts of "experts" had been unable to fix, and which had thus cost me a fortune.) But finally I
could abandon that ungrateful vehicle at Rimarko and turn my face
towards the mountains. I had new boots on my feet to keep out the
swamps and a rising excitement in my soul.

It was Guiseppi Barretti, who wrote, in 1760: "It is a great disadvantage not to be a botanist when one is travelling on foot." I
think that perhaps nothing gives me more pleasure than to be perched
at the brink of a new piece of alpine territory with an uninterrupted
stretch of botanizing before me. There were a suprising number of

flowers out above the tree line, far more than I noticed last year; I think most of them were over then, although the calendar time is much the same. Last June was much hotter and drier.

A lot of these plants were old friends from the Arctic, castaways from when the last ice age retreated. There were eight-petalled avens, various draba species, pink-flowered rock cresses, moss campions, snow buttercups, mountain marigolds, and an absolutely minute azalea with tiny point-petalled flowers. But most exciting of all, for I had never seen anything like it, was a small white flower on a stalk three-inches high. It

– spent deadhead late summer

– very early
– swamps & running creek above treeline & in subalpine clearings
– profuse

had six petals and two very oniony-looking leaves so I knew it had to be a lily. I could find only three specimens of this flower and they looked as if they were on their last legs. I looked it up as soon as I reached home, but none of my flower guides list it.

Instead of dropping down the big rock slide to Sam's cabin, I found a way to Fish Lake and picked up the old Horse Trail. The dog suddenly became very alert and interested in something ahead of us, but it didn't appear to be a bear, for she was not frightened. Large slabs of snow still striped the trail and on one of these I stumbled over wolf tracks. The day was dull and the wind keened steadily into my face, blurring my eyes with tears. Suddenly a flicker of movement caught my eye and there were two grey wolves, ragged and lean with summer. We stared at each other for a second, then they wheeled and disappeared over a rocky rise. Faintly on the wind, I heard the high yelping of puppies. But long before I reached a vantage point, the puppies had been stilled. A shallow rocky draw was then in front of me and the sweep of grey boulders that filled it was apparently as devoid of life as the moon.

In an attempt to avoid the river crossing in the canyon that I had made in the fall, and that would surely be impossible now that the river was so full, I kept much higher when I dropped off the plateau. I was saved by a foot log, an old, bleached spruce with many branches through which I wriggled and slithered, mostly on my seat, for the log was slick with spray. I had taken the dog's pack off so that she could negotiate the branches, but did not expect her to fall in, for she is usually sure-footed. But in she went: I watched in horror as she was swept into a frothing maelstrom of water. I threw my pack off and tried to get down the bank, but the brush was thick just there and I could not move quickly. Fortunately she was swept into an eddy and managed to hold her own; I could just reach her by hanging onto a branch and leaning over the water. Talk about a drowned rat — there is very little of Lonesome when she is not fluffed out by fur. She has nine lives, that dog. One year, at tree-planting camp, she nearly drowned in a culvert while pursuing ground squirrels (her only weakness); another year she met her first porcupine, an animal that is very rare here. And then there was last year's bear attack ...

Remembering the steep, broken country between the foot log and my lake, I tried to keep further west, but did not find a better route. Every time I paused to think and plan my way around the next obstacle, the bugs ate me alive; they were obviously anticipating the rain.

In the attic of the cabin, the squirrels had had a wonderful time. Boxes were ravaged and a trail of shredded cardboard led to their underground winter nests. One opportunistic creature had raided an opened bale of fibreglass batts; I found his summer home of grass and insulation halfway up a tree. The root cellar was the domain of mice and voles. Its insulation was riddled with holes and droppings and each of the potatoes that were left had a chunk bitten out of it.

The wharf, too, was a mess. The logs had been pushed up onto the rocks by high water. Fresh pollen rings on the rocks indicate that the lake has already dropped a foot. My first job was to wrestle the logs back in place with the come-along and peavey so that they would be ready for the plane.

But the plane has not come. The weather has deteriorated into fitful rain which rattles on the roof in staccato bursts and I don't suppose I'll see it now.

I have been sitting inside long enough. I think I'll take a turn around the swamp and see what's growing.

CHAPTER 19

June 30, 1989

I have been giving much thought to the location of my second cabin. The tip of the little point of land that was conceded to me by the Land Office is its highest part. There is a spot up there where I might be able to squeeze a cabin between the rocks, but to make it safe from falling trees, I would have to shave the promentory to the shoreline which would not only deprive me of shelter but also make a very ugly mess.

East of the bump is a small hollow which is, conversely, the most-sheltered part of the lease. By a stroke of pure luck, for when I built it I had considered only the way the rocks were arranged, the wharf happens to be where the hollow joins the lake. Often have I sat on the logs in relative calm while the tops of the trees tossed and writhed above me. Further proof of the shelter was the way the snow persisted last winter on the little balsams that inhabit the hollow, long after it was blown off the rest of the trees; also, the balsams here all had single leaders and grew without the sweeping skirts of branches indicative of exposed conditions.

But, the hollow was, as near as I could judge, outside the designated property, although it would have been well within the piece I originally applied for. Will the Land Office grant me an extension?

Should I even bother to apply for one and just plead ignorance? After all, it is not easy to measure over the rough ground with nothing but a tape; and the shoreline is so convoluted, it is difficult to determine exactly where the starting point should be.

Also, if I built in the hollow, I would have no view, certainly not of the western mountains and, unless I pruned a lot of trees to the east, no early morning sun. An alternative was to build on the slope between the hollow and the high point. Big, immovable boulders limited the choice of site there, but if I worked it right, I would be able to see the tops of the mountains through the west windows, be more open to the morning sun, yet still have a considerable amount of shelter. This site would be only partially out of my area — its main problem would be the slope. The foundations would have to be built up four feet at one side and braced so that the weight of the house would not push them down into the hollow; there was no way to secure them directly to the rocks short of using rock drills and cement, neither of which I was prepared to deal with. Also, with one side of the cabin floor so far off the ground, banking the walls with snow, at least in the early part of winter, would be a problem.

I could not seem to get started. It always takes me a day or two to settle down after I have been outside for a while. I poked around with the shovel at a few rocks, but did not want to disturb anything I did not have to. Besides, I had used all my camera film photographing flowers as I came over the pass and I wanted to take pictures of the site before I disturbed it — more film was coming on the plane.

The plane, when it did come, sneaking under a drizzly overcast, was a useful distraction, for sorting out the gear took a while. Then there was fuel to fetch from the crate and the saws to get ready and sharpen.

Then the sun came out, and suddenly everything was easy. I settled on the sloping site for the cabin, picked out the corners, and dug troughs to make space for the foundation logs that will be close to the ground. I felled all the trees on or close to the site and dragged them aside, and was even inspired to cut all their stumps flush with the ground, for the sooner the elements can get to work on the wounds, the quicker they will blend in with their surroundings.

And thus the second cabin is begun.

July 1, 1989

A pretty, soft, calm morning with golden mist rising from the lake. Ideal for tricky tree falling.

There were three large ones right on the waterfront that would have to come down. Two were tangled with each other and all but hung up on the dead snag that I want to preserve. The logistics of falling them had to be given considerable thought.

The westernmost tree was three paces away from the other two. At first, it had sought the light and so grown away from its overpowering neighbours, but when it grew higher than the shelter of the point and became influenced by Nuk Tessli, it promptly leaned the opposite way, becoming, in effect, banana-shaped. There were hefty-looking branches on two of the four sides and it was very difficult to determine its natural line of fall. I wanted to put it west, towards the point, as I wanted to use the trunk for lumber, and that would be the best place for me to deal with it. There were several other trees in that direction, any one of which was big enough to snarl my tree, but I am glad to say, as much by luck as judgement, it came down exactly where I wanted it, breaking off only one neighbouring branch on its way. So far so good.

Tree number two was a monster with a great, flaring butt through which even the longest bar on the chain saw could not reach. It was destined to make lumber, too, and I figured that if I could fall it on the rocks along the waterfront, the lumber-making process could be conducted there. Hopefully next year's high water would wash the mess away. The gods must have been smiling at me because once again the tree landed on target.

I had no choice with the third one, for it had a very strong lean directly over the wharf; I brought it down right across the wharf logs, wondering if they would break; but they held firm. Trees one and two were white-barks, but number three was a lodgepole. I walked out onto it and cut off all the branches that I could reach, dragging each one into land as soon as it was free, for I didn't want to leave them littering the water. The saw seems to work quite happily in the water, although the operator, if she cannot get out of the way, must weather great gouts of water thrown up by the chain. It was interesting to note that while the water surface was thick with needles, I had perfect balance on the log, but as soon as the branches were cleared away and the drop into the water could be seen, I could move only one limb at a time, like a chameleon, gripping like grim death with the other three. What tricks our eyes play on us.

The branches from tree number two, however, are not in the way and they can stay there for the time being. The little fish that live around the wharf are enjoying their new, green feathery canyons. I was not too happy about the scum of sawdust and its attendant rainbow squiggles of chain oil, but the lake is so far very forgiving; in a few hours, the water around the wharf was as sweet and clean as ever.

I have decided to build this cabin a little differently from the other. I will still use a version of the piece-on-piece method, but instead of solid logs for the fillers, I will use half logs with the rounded portion outside; inside, the walls will be lined with store-bought lumber and there will be a layer of fibreglass in between. It will certainly cost a lot more money to buy and fly in the extra man-made materials, but it will save many trees in the area as well as giving me a lot less clean-up to do. I have lived with log walls for a number of years now; it was fun for a while, but I find them rather overbearing and busy on the whole. I like my interiors to be as light and neutral as possible so that they don't compete too much with the magnificence outside.

I can afford to be a lot more objective about this cabin. Not only have I a much better idea of what I am doing, but I also already have a good shelter in which to live. The new cabin is to be bigger; it will be fifteen-feet wide and twenty-feet long, which will mean an extra section of wall for each side. The porch will be on the north, rather than the south, end; it should thus give far more protection to the door. Because the inside of the cabin is to be built with foreign materials only, all outer surfaces can be left unpeeled, which should save a little time although hauling some of the bigger logs might be more difficult that way.

Two jobs must be tackled fairly quickly: one is to hunt up and peel all the roof components so that they will be as light as possible when I am ready for them. The other is to make enough floorboards to cover the foundations; mindful of the eyebrow incident and the greater irregularity of ground at this site, I am going to have to have a solid platform on which to work.

July 2, 1989

It took quite a while to decide the best way to buck up the tree that lay on the rocks. Only the middle was suitable for full-length floor-boards and the sections around it had to be coaxed away so that there would be room for the mill. As these pieces were very heavy and the water was on one side and a steep jump onto the bank on the other, there was a lot of messing about and cursing and swearing (quietly, in deference to my dog) before that was accomplished.

It helps to file saw teeth straight across for lumber-making and I have three of these chains, one worn to the nubs and the other two not much better. I chose the most likely one, but its rakers needed filing down; so that took time. Then I put it on the saw and bolted on the mill, a tedious process that involves much skinning of knuckles because, as with most machines, the nuts are in an awkward place. But when I fired it up, it refused to cut at all. I had put the chain on backwards. I thought I had grown out of that a long time ago. So off the mill had to come again, with more loss of skin; the chain had to be flipped, the bar put on, and then, once more, the mill.

During which, I dropped the wrench that I was using to tighten the nuts into the lake. The tool had disturbed underwater debris, which floated in a cloud and hid it. Balancing as best I could on nearby rocks that broke the surface, I reached down into a slimy crevice to see if I could find the wrench; when my arm was in the water to the shoulder, my fingers just touched the handle. I was lucky: with all the bottomless cavities beneath me, I could easily never have seen the wrench again and I did not have a spare.

Now the saw should work. But it moved so laboriously through the tree, that it took two full tanks of gas to cut off the slab, when a third of a tank should have sufficed. The chain was so tight it would barely move in its groove. The only way to get at the bar tightening nut was to take the mill completely off again....

But still it was not cutting properly. The depth control slipped as the saw progressed. One side of the board became two inches thick instead of the planned one and a quarter (the floorboards for the first cabin being much thicker than necessary). The depth control cannot be tightened indefinitely, for it will strip and snap. That happened once and it is such an odd size that I have been unable to find a spare. (This is an old model, I should imagine that newer ones are better serviced.) But I readjusted it and tried again. This time the mill wanted to climb out of the log. It meant that the bar was too worn. I took the mill off again (the less said about that the better), looked at the bar but could not see any obvious deformity, flipped it over, replaced the mill, and tried again. Finally, I had a board: but on the next cut, the problem was just as bad. There was nothing for it but to abandon lumber-making for the time being and put a new bar and chain on my shopping list for next time I go out.

And that was the end of the day. To show for it, I had: one outer slab, part of which will form a filler; one floorboard; and four sore knuckles.

July 10, 1989

We are having peculiar weather. It is windless and, periodically, we are treated to deluges of rain. I hear the approaching roar of these cataracts and dive for the cabin. They may last a few minutes or as much as a couple of hours; sometimes the sun breaks through and illuminates the silver lances of rain, turning it all to steam. It is more like living in a tropical rainforest than five thousand feet up on the dry side of a mountain range. The radio says these warm air streams are coming up from Hawaii: I'd be just as happy if they stayed there.

The no-see-ums, however, are loving it. They are not foiled by the mosquito screens and gather in thousands at the bottoms of the windows; they climb up a little way and drop back in a never-ending motion, round and round, rather like those mesmerizing moving sculptures in art galleries.

Last year, hummingbirds occasionally buzzed the red fuel cans by the camp. Apparently they live on tree sap and insects when there is not enough nectar, in fact they feed their young on them.

Suburban birds of any breed are so programmed to feeders, that they will come at once if you hang one up. In places where wild birds are not accustomed to them, it may take years before they recognize the artificial food and learn what the feeder is for. So when I hung my hummingbird feeder up against the kitchen window, I did not expect much. But within twenty minutes, a hummingbird was there. Within an hour, there were two of them, one a male and the other a female, fighting furiously over the plastic blossoms.

There is not a lot of sun with this calm, warm air mass, but canoeing can be very beautiful in the still, grey-green mornings. How gracefully the branches of pine and balsam swoop, dip, and cling to the rocks along the shore. The spicy Labrador tea is in flower, as are the dwarf, shrubby mats of the swamp laurel. Here, this plant never grows more than

a few inches high and the flowers are no bigger than a small pea. The buds look remarkably like pink whorls of icing squeezed out of bags by cake decorators. This is because each petal has a curious little bump which protrudes outwards near its centre. The bump is a pocket that stores a pollen-laden anther. When the flower opens, the anther remains in its pocket and its stalk, or filament, becomes stretched like a bow. When touched, it flies up and wallops the intruder, thus ensuring the pollen is carried to the next flower. I should imagine it is like walking on an automatic powderpuff with powder grains the size of tennis balls. I suppose an insect cannot mind this treatment too much, however, or it would not continue to land on the same kind of flower.

The conifers are blooming now as well. The lodgepole pines have yellow pollen cones, but the white-barks are bright red; before they open, they look like berries. The fir's flowers, both male and female, are an amazing, deep blue. Why should this be? Colour is generally assumed to be an attraction for a fertilizing animal, but conifers are wind-pollinated. What an enormous amount of pollen is produced. It flies like smoke when the wind blows and accumulates in fascinating swirls on sheltered pools and at the edges of the lakes.

My canoe trips must be limited as there is so much to do, but one morning I went as far as the beach near the other end of the lake, where Richard brought my first load of equipment. In April, when I snowshoed by there, I found a beer bottle stuck up in a tree and wanted to make sure there had been no garbage hidden under the snow.

What a strange mentality it is to apparently enjoy the bush but have no compunction about strewing it with garbage. Why do such people go into the bush? If it is the "wilderness experience," why can they not see that their actions are destroying it? With its mouth placed carefully over a twig, this particular bottle was not plain thoughtlessness, but a deliberate statement. Whoever had done it was probably saying, "This is Me! Mighty Hunter! Wilderness Tamer!"

"Mighty Garbage Man," more like.

I work and work, but as nothing has been done to the cabin site itself, I seem to be getting nowhere. Almost all my activities have been in the swamp where I have been finding, falling, and peeling the roof components. I also dragged in six long, unpeeled logs, two for the foundations and four for the floor joists. It was a slow and painful operation, these logs being heavier than any I have hauled in to date; it took most of two days.

I am going out tomorrow. I have been here only two weeks, but I have to go to Williams Lake to pick up more lumber and the roofing for the second cabin, which I ordered when I drove through after tree-planting. It will take several trips to fetch everything I need.

On the way out, I will start to ribbon from the far side of my lake and try once more to find a better route to the high valley. The ribboning will slow me down and I will carry an overnight camp with me.

I might just be lucky with the weather, for this evening the clouds have broken and the sky is full of gentle golds. There are silver rings on the lake where the fish are feeding and a hermit thrush is singing brightly in the glass-clear air.

CHAPTER 20

July 19, 1989

I saw a bear on the way out, just above the foot-log (which Lonesome crossed without incident this time). The bear ran away at once, but not before I had a good look at it; it was another funny-coloured "black" bear, having sharply contrasting flecks of white all over it and perfect halos of white fur around each ear. The bear ran off in the direction I wanted to go so I made a large detour, hoping that the bear did not have the same idea.

Thus I arrived at yet another lake that I had not seen before. It was perhaps a mile long and fairly regular in shape; it had such a lovely view of the mountains at the head of it that I resolved to include it permanently on my route. I still don't have maps of this area; the stores in Williams Lake don't stock them and it seems as though I shall have to send away to Ottawa for them.

I was close to the point where I had seen the wolves when I heard the click of a metal-shod hoof on stone. It was Bob and Patrick. "We knew it had to be you," said Patrick. "We might occasionally see a hiker's bootprints along here, but never ones with dog paw marks so neatly in the tracks!"

Bob and Francie's camp was about a mile away and a visit could not be passed up. I told them about the new lake I had just encountered and asked them if they had a name for it. "That's Round Lake," Bob said. Francie laughed and added: "We are not very original with our lake names, we've got several Round Lakes."

"Wasn't it you who named my lake, Square Lake?" I said to Bob. He nodded and I asked him why, because it did not seem remotely square to me.

To which he replied, with no trace of guile, "Because it wasn't round."

There is a sawmill in Nimpo Lake that processes local trees, but it makes lumber for export only. In Williams Lake I discovered a family-owned business that not only had the lumber I wanted, but was prepared to deliver it. And what is more, as it was not a full load, the truck driver said he would be glad to pick up anything else I wanted in Williams Lake for no extra charge. This was wonderful news for he could handle all the heavy roofing and I would not have to make any more trips into town.

I hiked back over the mountains on one of those vivid days when cloud and sun alternate and shadows fly over the hills. The second flowering was close to its peak and the meadows were a riot of colour. The gems on that trip were a dwarf forget-me-not with dense clusters of vivid cobalt blue flowers and an alpine lupin with racimes no longer than an inch; it looked more like a blue and white clover. Each of its tiny, silvery palmate leaves would not have covered my thumbnail.

It looks as though we are going to have another good day. There is some cloud but it is coming from the east and the lake is shimmering and luminous. The cabin awaits me. The components for the foundation are hauled; all I have to do is figure out how to put them together.

July 23, 1989

Raising the first corner post of the basement was no problem at all — it was only four-feet long and I simply lifted it in my arms and sat it on its end on top of a flattish rock that happened to be in the right place. But keeping it there while the end of the first foundation log was lifted onto it was something else. Too late, I realized I should not have been so efficient and cut off all the stumps, for now I had no anchors for braces.

The log was part of the big lodgepole I had fallen over the wharf. My first attempt to lift it was a failure. I thought a skid and the come-along would be enough, but the log snubbed against the top of the post when it had but an inch to go and was far too heavy for me to move the remaining distance. As I was contemplating this, the nail holding the skid gave way and the log crashed down, narrowly missing my toes. So a gin pole it had to be. A rafter was commissioned, guyed elaborately to the little balsams, and up came the log.

Only one end needed to be on a post, the other, because of the slope of the ground, rested on a rock. The log at the other end of the cabin was treated in like fashion and both were soon permanently braced in a way that I hope will prevent them from sliding down the slope. All the other logs could then be dragged onto the slope above the site and rolled down into place.

With a new bar and chain for the big saw, the floorboards peeled off the tree at the waterfront with comparative ease. I laid them unedged and upside down, so that the worst side would bear all the construction dirt. I needed far more than the log on the rocks could provide me and back to the swamp I had to go and fall more trees.

As always when I go out, I had booked a plane load of supplies to follow my own arrival. I could have all my stuff flown in at once, I suppose, but by staggering the planes, I can have fresh vegetables each time one comes. Besides, I have nowhere to store such things as roofing and lumber on this uneven ground without spending time to build platforms.

On this latest plane came a bag of lime. Some was to be used to sweeten the outhouse, but some was for my little pocket of garden. I had heard that wood ash was good for the soil, too, and I took a bucket of it and another of lime and dug them into the cold, swampy ground. I gave it twenty-four hours to settle then put in little rows of raddishes, lettuces, cress, spinach, and chard. The very next day, I read in my latest *Harrowsmith* magazine, that wood ash might prevent some minerals from being available and that lime inhibited growth for six weeks. Six weeks! That is the bulk of my growing season. I guess I'm never going to be much of a gardener.

July 28, 1989

We are having some dramatic thunderstorms. I can see them build up over Maydoe Pass as I work; the sky turns a prune-plum blue, thunder bangs and grumbles all about the heavens, and the hills disappear in solid walls of water. The mountains in the west often stay clear and, as the sun drops lower, it shoots livid beams beneath the storm clouds, lighting the islands eerily and spectacularly: chartreuse ships in a prune-plum sea.

The radio says there have already been six hundred fires in British Columbia this year. Apparently, there is a new computer method for detecting lightning strikes. The program records each air-to-ground, i.e., positive strike, but ignores cloud-to-cloud, or negative, ones. There have been five hundred positive strikes in the mid Coast District so far this month, but only two have resulted in fires due to the heavy rains that fell with them. If this proportion of strikes to fires has been duplicated province-wide, the mind boggles at the number of strikes necessary to produce six hundred fires. What a different summer this is from last year.

The mountain that dominates the view from this cabin reminds me of a photograph in my art history book of a painting by François Boucher, completed in 1752. It is of a young and pretty, naked woman arranged sexily on her stomach on a couch. She was one of Louis XV's mistresses, reputedly an Irish lass by the name of "Louise O'Murphy." The three-peaked mountain in front of the cabin, with two bumps to the left, one to the right, and a saddle in between, has exactly the profile of Louise O'Murphy's back, shoulders, and buttocks.

One morning, it was excessively hot and cloudless, without a breath of wind. The lake was polished steel and the air as brittle as crystal, each sun-edged pine needle diamond hard. The little minnows by the wharf jumped and skittered, but their silver ripples were extinguished instantly. Sounds echoed across the water. The snap of a tiny twig was a handclap; my voice rattled strangely inside my head. The dog was exceedingly nervous, starting at every little thing.

When the storm came, it was almost a relief. Blue-black clouds swallowed Fish Lake and a great column of lightning, thick as a tree, hit Louise O'Murphy right between the shoulder blades.

What a dilly that must have registered on the computers. I expected walls of fire to erupt or, at the very least, the mountain to shiver into fragments. But after the rain cleared and I could see it properly again, it seemed just as before. As the thunder died away, Louise O'Murphy blushed a deep, rose red all down her flanks and a double rainbow arched above her in the sky.

CHAPTER 21

August 1, 1989

The cabin has suddenly leapt into existence.

None of the short uprights were difficult to raise; trimmed, they were light enough to lift without a gin pole. Being able to work on a solid floor made a difference, too, for no longer was I balancing on stray rocks or doing the splits on the floor joists. After the short uprights came the two fifteen-foot end posts: as before, the setup to erect them was time consuming, but the posts themselves rose predictably and smoothly. The tie logs and the ceiling joists followed; unfortunately, they have not dried out as much as I had hoped because they have lain in the swamp. Many have become blackened in places with mould. This is always a risk with summer-peeled logs if they are not immediately put in a sunny, well-aired place. The mould can never be completely removed.

When I first occupied the lease, I earmarked three particularly tall, straight lodgepoles for the ridgepole and plate logs of this cabin, each of which have to be twenty-nine-feet long. It was an interesting business to haul them, trying to manipulate them between all the rocks and trees on the way. In some respects, a longer log is easier to haul than a shorter one; once it is on the rocks, it touches the ground in only one or two places, consequently the friction is less. However,

it rarely stays nicely on top of the rocks but usually rolls down and wedges itself in a gap.

Using the slope of the ground above the cabin, the plate logs were very easy to roll onto the structure and they have already been fitted. But now I have come to a halt as far as the frame of the building is concerned. The ceiling boards, the tongue-and-groove cottonwood that I bought in Williams Lake, have not yet been flown in (the lumber had not arrived in Nimpo when my last flight was booked). It would be possible, but difficult and not a little danger-ous, to raise the ridgepole and rafters without ceiling boards to stand on, so I prefer to wait.

I feel well pleased with myself at the smooth progress to date. The new-cut, golden wood is splendid against the blue sparkle of the lake. Beyond the cabin, Louise O'Murphy smiles or glowers, implacable or moody as she thinks fit.

My next project will be the walls. It will be some time before I see any progress there, however, because most of the fillers still have to be made. It is pointless cutting them without also slicing the logs from which the wider ones will be taken into lumber. I will need a large quantity of shorter boards, not only for the two porch floors and the gable ends, but also for a walkway around the east wall of the cabin, an open deck facing the lake, and eventually, a new, improved wharf. I dread the thought of all that lumber-making. The new bar and chain are cutting well, but the motor of the saw is not behaving. It has been racing and then quitting — I give it a shake, it usually starts alright, works well for a while, then races and quits again.

August 5, 1989

It is my birthday. I am forty-two years old. Most of my contemporaries have conventional careers, long-established families, grandchildren, even. But here I am, playing with my Lego set, my piggy bank almost empty, and I love it.

August 18, 1989

Lumber-making became so frustrating with the ailing saw I decided to take it to Bella Coola. There are no good saw mechanics that I know of around Nimpo, for all the logging there is done by feller-bunchers, monstrous machines that look like a cross between a brontosaurus and a lamprey eel. But in the valley, where, because of the steep ground and massive trees all logging is done with saws, good mechanics abound.

But the trip to Bella Coola had mixed results. Because of the sudden hot, dry weather, logging had been stopped. Everyone connected with the business went away on holiday, including all the saw mechanics.

I took my leaking truck to a man who knows it well; I sometimes think he would go out of business if it wasn't for all the work I give him. He looked long and hard at the transfer case (as all the other "experts" had done before him) and said that he didn't think the problem was the seal (which had been replaced three times) but that the oil was being shoved out of the vent. Why, he didn't know. He thought that if he put a sleeve on the vent, the extruded oil might fall back into the transfer case. So he clamped on three inches of rubber hose, for which he did not even charge — and it worked.

Another man who worked at the garage looked at the chain saw although he said he did not know a lot about them. He fiddled with the carburettor, said, rather patronizingly, that condensation was my problem, and pronounced it OK. It still doesn't sound quite right to me. It seems to be running too fast but I have been using it at low power for so long, perhaps I have forgotten what it should sound like.

A great bonus to the valley trip were the gardens. Everyone is overflowing with too many vegetables. I spent several happy hours grazing down rows and have begged what I can to bring up with me; it should be arriving with the ceiling boards and the chain saw, at any moment.

Also coming on the plane will be all my remaining wild flower books, which were stored in the valley. I dug them out to see if I could find any reference to the little alpine lily that had excited me on my first trip over the top this year. None of my North American volumes listed it, but in the bottom of the box was the *Concise British Flora* by W. Keble Martin, which I have had since I was a child. Many flowers, particularly the alpine ones, are circumpolar. I flipped the book open idly (it smelled of must and storage), focussed my eyes where they fell in the centre of one of the crowded plates — and there it was. It is known as the mountain spiderwort in Britain and is apparently extremely rare there, but much commoner in both Alaska and the European Alps, where it is called the alp lily.

So I haven't exactly discovered a new species, but it is obviously not a well-known plant and the speculation and detective work were a lot of fun.

I consolidated much of the new high valley route on the journeys back and forth, and "discovered" yet more interesting flowers. One was a green-flowered orchid which was a little unusual because it was growing on a dry gravel slope rather than the boggy or shady places most northern orchids prefer. I think, from my books, it is an Alaskan orchid, but I will have to look at the details of the flowers much more closely before that can be confirmed.

The hummingbirds have gone. Before I left, I filled the feeder and hung it high in the eaves of the porch to keep it out of reach of any stray bears, but it was hardly touched. The weather is beautiful this morning, but the seasons are getting ready to turn and I am anxious to get on with the cabin. Where are you, Richard?

CHAPTER 22

August 24, 1989

The saw is still not running well; it is racing and quitting and sometimes now it is difficult to start. If, when it falters, I can pull the choke out a fraction, that helps quite a bit, but I have to be fast. The choke won't stay at that point by itself so I have had to train my left hand to hold the trigger and throttle of the saw with three fingers and have the thumb and first finger poised ready on the choke. Lumber-making has turned into its usual grinding torment.

There is now an appalling mess along the waterfront, for it is the two trees on the rocks that I have been tackling. The rocks are knee deep in sawdust and most of the branches are, by now, waterlogged and excruciatingly heavy. They have become covered in a slimy growth which floats free in greenish strands under water, but looks like gobs of clear jelly when brought into the air. I suppose it is an algae. The branches will have to be yanked in and lopped off a bit at a time as they are far too heavy to drag up all at once. There is already a distinctive chill to the water that I will have to work in up to my waist much of the time, but if I don't do the job soon, I will still have the mess next summer. So I will tackle that next; it will give me a few hours' break from the saw.

The huckleberry crop greatly exceeds that of last year. Huckle-

berries are probably one of the com-
monest plants in the forest's sparse
understorey, but most bushes seem to
be sterile. There are dozens of species
in the huckleberry family, many difficult to identify. Some of mine are
obviously different — I have two with
much bluer berries, one with fat, shiny
black berries, another with tiny purple
fruit. I would love to be able to sort
out the species, but that will take the
kind of time I cannot afford right
now.

My stomach enjoys the huckleberries
without being so particular as to spe-
cies. I simply cannot harvest and preserve any this year, but I eat a
bowlful for my supper and put them into what I think of as "cake,"
an eggless, multigrained mixture of nuts and fruit sweetened with
molasses, generally very heavy, but which, I console myself as I chew
my way through it, is probably very good for me.

I have been invaded by mice. Never was so much death occa-
sioned for so little money as with my two ninety-nine-cent traps. It's
a pity that the little creatures become so destructive, for they are
attractive animals, but my man-made environment suits them very
well and they have taken over with a vengeance.

Most of the creatures I catch are, according to *The Provincial
Museum of British Columbia: Mammals*, white-footed, or deer, mice.
The book informs me that subspecies about the province have a
great variation in size, colour, length of tail, etc. It details *Peromyscus
maniculatus alpinus* for my area, stating that this is the only subspecies that lives over four-thousand feet, and describes it as having a
tail longer than head and body combined. However, my mice have
tails barely as long as the body alone: perhaps I can call it *Peromyscus
maniculatus alpinus var. nuk tesslii.*

August 26, 1989

I have come to another ignominious halt. Just behind the cabin is a
great, uprooted white-bark which has been down long enough for

the bark to disintegrate and the trunk to weather a silver grey. There was a small bit of rot in one place, but it seemed only superficial and I thought I could probably wangle two eight-foot lengths from it, which would give me four large wall slabs and a good number of boards. I rigged up the guide board and the mill, but halfway through the first cut, there was a big bang and the saw stopped dead.

I knew at once that that was it. Final. I pulled the string a few times, changed the plug, and took the carburettor apart and put it together again, just in case such incomprehensible magic might work, but nothing. The pulling sounded different: there was no life to it.

I have several alternatives. I can go out immediately and see if I can find anyone to fix it. The Bella Coola loggers may still not be home from their vacations — I suppose it depends on the weather when they will work again. The nearest saw shop otherwise is Williams Lake; if I drive there myself I might be lucky enough to find someone to mend it while I waited, but it would still take several days and the thought of another dreary drive to town does not appeal to me at all. A bus runs twice a week, as does a courier service, and I could dispatch the saw that way and make long-distance arrangements by phone. But that will still mean long thumb-twiddling waits in Nimpo.

Richard is due in five days; if I decide to go out I must arrive at Nimpo before that time to postpone the flight.

Which gives me three days here. If I wanted to rig up a scaffold on the ceiling joists, I could put up the ridgepole. I suppose the rafters could go up, too, but they will hang over the tops of the walls and make it difficult to fit the last of the fillers. I could also make a start on tidying up the awful mess of branches that is lying all over the property. Or I could do more work on the trail over the roughest part of the ridge just south of my lake. I have been looking at it and think I might try a spur even further to the west than any I have yet attempted. If I am away, however, it would be just my luck to have an unscheduled visitor. (A couple of recreational fliers have already dropped by this year. The pilots saw the activity and assumed the buildings were a fishing lodge; they were both somewhat nonplussed when I told them the fish were plentiful but small and not considered good "sport." One man even had the crassness to say: "What on earth is there to do up here then?") A visitor might not be able to do much, but they could at least take the saw out for me and save me backpacking it. Perhaps I can leave the saw on the wharf with a message on it just in case.

People think I lead a simple life.

August 28, 1989

It would make a very tedious document to record all the ups and downs and backwarding and forwarding I did before I eventually found a far more acceptable route across the south ridge. Suffice it to say that the dog became extremely weary; whenever I backtracked to pick up ribbons or try a different route, she would look at me as if to say, "Now, are you really sure this time?" The route that I have finalized has probably added even more distance to the trip, but it is so much more pleasant, it is worth it.

I stood, for the first time, on the shore of Octopus Lake from which runs the southern branch of Whitton Creek. It takes about two hours to reach Octopus Lake from here. Octopus Lake is definitely not round: it has a mass of arms and inlets, some are actually separate bodies of water from the main lake but the whole lot is so confusing from the ground it is hard to distinguish which is which. At its outlet, where one of the arms is too narrow for a lake but not yet quite a river, there is a possible crossing place. It is shallow and floored with smallish rocks although there seems to be a narrow, deeper channel in the middle. It will mean a wet crossing again, but what with swamps and other water wading, my feet are rarely dry on the trip to the road in any case.

All the ribbons I had placed between the lake shore and the foot-log were now obsolete. As I was out of flagging tape, I would have to collect those markers before I could define the new route. By following the river down, it was not difficult to find the foot-log. I sat beside it, consuming a sandwich from which most of the molasses had run, not only out of the bread, but through a hole in the plastic bag and into my pocket. I imagined it dripping out by slow degrees all the way through the bush and a hungry bear following the tasty trail, licking up the drops.

No fairy godmother materialized and so I will leave tomorrow and backpack the saw out to Rimarko. I am sitting on my wharf as I write this, watching the dying sun illuminate much of the country I will cross tomorrow. I shall have to canoe quite a way up the lake before I start hiking. I have to imagine most of the route to Octopus Lake as it is hidden from here, but the canyon into which the river falls below the outlet is visible by its shadow. From there Louise O'Murphy begins to rise: the Horse Trail runs right between her buttocks. Fish Lake is hidden by Big Island, but the mountain east of it (home of the alp lily) peeps over the top, far to my left.

A large number of dragonflies have suddenly appeared. Big ones with irridescent blue diamonds on their finger-length bodies. Their mating seems a drastic affair. Two insects fly along each busy with their own pursuits, then suddenly, like two magnets, they crash together. There is a furious clattering and buzzing of wings and arching of bodies as each animal seems to want nothing more than its own personal freedom. Then suddenly they pop apart and all is calm again. My books tell me that these creatures are a very early form of life and have remained completely unchanged for millions of years. Except that at one time, they grew to four feet in length. Did they mate in that way then? Whizzing and crashing about in the steamy young coal forests?

That must have been a sight to see.

September 5, 1989

The whole world is a balmy blue; blue sky, a blue lake so gently ruffled that it is a web of light. Hung in the upside-down sky, close to the mountains, is the small, dark shape of a man in a canoe.

It is Hans. He is a young German visiting Canada for the summer. How he wound up at Barbie and Alex's, where even the dog isn't particularly enamoured of men, I didn't enquire too closely.

Hans can fix anything. He has repaired all sorts of dilapidated machinery at the ranch, even the gas-operated washing machine that now, on command, quivers and belches water on the beach in front of the cabin and saves the family tedious trips to the laundromat at Anahim Lake. Hans delved into the slick, oily bowels of my chain saw and, rather in the manner of Jack Horner with his plum, fished out the piston. "See," he said, "you have a deep scratch in it, that is why you have no compression. I can probably make a temporary repair, but it would be better to buy new parts."

I drove out to Nimpo, but the store told me the parts would take at least a week to get there. So Hans spent a few hours rubbing the piston with emery paper and, lo and behold, the saw worked again. I ran off a couple of tanks of gas bucking up firewood at Rimarko to give it a bit of a trial, but it would be the lumber-making that would be the real test. So what else could I do but persuade Mr. Fixit to come back with me.

I don't think he took a lot of persuading, because mountains are one of his passions. He is, perforce, an excellent hiker. We pioneered yet more new country on the way home and yesterday I took him up in the direction of the North Pass. I was more than anxious to see what lay below the smooth covering of snow over which I had snowshoed in March.

I was not disappointed: the ground was free of brush and major obstacles — a little boggy in places but nothing serious. It will make an easy tourist hike. Moreover, as much as I can determine from the lateness of the season, it appears to be an excellent flower area; if that was not enough, the Coast Mountains arrange themselves behind the meadows in classic calendar-picture fashion.

Hans and I did not climb "Snowshoe Mountain" but crossed the North Pass (now blue with its promised lakes) and over another ridge with still more lakes and another valley beyond. At the head of this valley was an eight-and-a-half-thousand-foot mountain on the Tweedsmuir Park boundary; from its summit we were able to see many of the topographical features clustered around my old cabin at the Atnarko. We were poised above the great north-south Atnarko trough and could see the upper parts of the creeks as they tumbled down into it from the glaciers but the bottom was hidden from us by a shelf of land.

We probably travelled for ten hours with very little rest. Hans told me of similar long days he had spent in the European Alps where he might have climbed two peaks instead of one — but the distances between them would have been travelled by train or cable car through valleys filled with people. A very different concept from here.

CHAPTER 23

September 11, 1989

Yesterday, there was an ominous, hazy cast to the light as the sun rose. A storm? It was very warm.

It was soon obvious that smoke was the cause. The atmosphere thickened and before long I could barely see across the lake. Above the smog, the sun blazed, but it was so veiled that I could look it straight in the eye. It was deathly still and oppressively hot. The lake had an oily look: the silver sparks created by the jumping fish were instantly extinguished.

About twenty miles to the northeast, behind the rash of summer cabins on the far side of Charlotte Lake, are the great clear-cuts made by the company that has erected the mill near Nimpo. If there was any movement of air at all, it was coming from this direction. Were they slash- burning in this hot, dry weather? Would that make so much smoke? Was it a wildfire? Would anyone think about me and come and rescue me if it was coming my way? Would they be able to? Visibility was so poor I doubted anyone could fly, in fact I heard not a sound of a plane all day.

Oh for a radiophone. I have not been able to consider buying a new one, but friends of mine who have one are shortly going to leave the bush and I may be able to do a trade with them. However, that was not much use now.

If a fire was coming my way, my salvation would have to be the lake. I put a few possessions into a pile in the middle of the cabin floor; camping gear, journals, exposed films, a couple of irreplaceable books, and slid the canoe to the water and tied it to the wharf. All day, as I worked, I found myself stopping, looking, and listening.

The air cleared a little towards the evening and I paddled out into the lake where I could get a better look at what was going on. Billows of brown smoke coiled and roiled behind the North Ridge like a great, silent, Chinese dragon. There was no sound bar the little plops of fish and the distant murmur of the river as it ran out of the lake.

During the night, I woke with a jerk, convinced I smelled smoke. I ran outside, expecting to see the horizon in flames, but the smell was either a stray eddy from the chimney or a dream, for the night was clear, the stars brilliant, the air clean and sweet.

This morning there is a fresh breeze from the west, the mountains are hard-edged and sharp, and the fireball of the sun can no longer be faced. There is not a scrap of smoke to be seen. My pile of possessions on the floor looks a little ridiculous.

I wonder what that was all about?

September 13, 1989

The Indian summer goes on and on. The mornings are so clear and still, were it not for the faint murmur of the river, the whack of a cone dropped by a squirrel, or the tick of the cabin roof responding to the sun, I would seriously doubt the viability of my ears. The tiniest of sounds come to me across the lake. Yesterday there was a series of constipated grunts, apparently the love poem of a bull moose to an amorous female; she must have been there, too, for the grunting was followed by a low, cowlike moo.

The other day, the quiet was disrupted by four of the most bloodcurdling shrieks, the last of which faded away in a gurgle, a classic horror-movie sound effect. Something got eaten, no doubt.

But what got eaten?

And what ate?

September 16, 1989

I am at exactly the same stage with the building as I was on this day last year, about to brace the end posts to the ridgepole. That memorable occasion marked the arrival of the first great dump of snow. Two days ago, I would have said that snow was a long way from happening this year, for the 14th was another in an endless series of cloudless, blue days, with the underbrush a breathless gold and only the faintest tang of fall in the air. But yesterday I shivered as a cold, northwest wind blew through my open window holes and today the mountains dissolved in veils of cloud which, as they reached me, were full of falling pellets of hissing, frozen snow. But this was snow as it ought to be at this time of year, a skiff, a warning, and gone.

The afternoon deteriorated into gusts of rain and sleety showers, but nothing settled on the ground. I dragged the old, blue tarp onto the ceiling boards (which were flown in on the plane that picked up Hans and laid prior to erecting the ridgepole) in the hope that most of whatever came out of the sky would be diverted.

Gradually all the hills about me were socked in right down to lake level, but just before I left the building site, driven in early by the miserable weather, the clouds to the south swirled briefly apart. There was Louise O'Murphy, mysterious and unfamiliar, in a dazzling, new, winter-white gown.

September 18, 1989

In the morning, the trees were spangled with moisture of that peculiar texture that is not quite water and not quite ice. A stray handful of huckleberries still hung on a bush; they were juicy and tangy with the ice-water droplets on them.

The tarp had been a waste of time; it was full of holes and it still retained puddles which were dripping monotonously and familiarly into the box of the room below.

Very gradually, the soft, snow-vague clouds pulled apart and then suddenly it was the most gorgeous and dreamy afternoon imaginable. The air was a hazy blue, the lake still and windless. Louise O'Murphy was no longer smoothly white, but splotched and freckled. The big mountains were featureless and opaque with the sun behind them and the smoke-blue water below them was marked occasionally by dazzling streaks where a loon or a finger of wind tracked the surface.

I have to go to Nimpo tomorrow; I seem to have spent my whole summer trotting back and forth. It is voting day again, this time a by-election.

If the weather is bad in the morning, I will have to forgo the Octopus Lake route and go down to Sam's cabin; from there I can make the decision to either go down the river and around Charlotte Lake, or take a chance at the big rock slide and Maydoe Pass. I have not been to Sam's cabin yet this year; I wonder if the bear has been back?

September 25, 1989

He had. Before I left in April, I had pounded heavy bolts of wood over the windows of the cabin and wired the door in three places. That had foiled the bear quite satisfactorily — so he'd pulled down the wall.

September 29, 1989

I am burning out. On the whole, apart from the couple of days' sleet, the weather has been wonderful and I should be able to work from dawn to dusk. But it is a real effort to make myself start in the morning and I find myself frequently staring blankly into space as the day grinds on.

I am back to my usual occupation of lugging stuff in from the swamp. It is the strapping I am carrying now, for the remaining rafters have been notched in.

I am not the only creature hauling material endlessly back and forth: the squirrels are busy storing their winter provender. One animal was walking so awkwardly, I rested my own burden and stopped to look at him. The object he was carrying looked like a piece of old black leather at least as large as he was. It was a dried mushroom, a double one with two fruiting bodies branching from the bottom.

Squirrels are marvellously engineered animals — which other creature can hurtle down a vertical surface at full speed and stop dead? This squirrel obviously had mapped out the brush and other debris around the cabin, for he knew where he wanted to go, but his prize was not being co-operative and it would not fit into the small spaces he was accustomed to using. After considerable contortions and pushings and shovings on his part (and how I sympathized with him), he ran up a short twig on top of a brushpile, apparently expecting to be able to leap from it to a small balsam. He suddenly realized he wasn't going to make it and teetered on the brink. There was nothing for it but to drag, bully, and cajole the mushroom into the bowels of the brushpile, then fight his way up the slim trunk of the tree. A whorl of branches provided another obstacle and it was here that tragedy struck. The mushroom was wrested from the squirrel's grasp and it fell to the ground. Down went the squirrel to retrieve it, appearing again in a moment to hang his booty in the forked branch where it belonged. He paused and chittered most proudly at his accomplishment; but, poor creature, what he did not realize was that the double mushroom had broken and all he had was the smaller of the fruiting bodies. I wondered if he would be aware of this and go and retrieve the much larger piece, but he ran off in a different direction altogether. He obviously cannot count.

The last green flush was still in the sky behind the mountains and I was reading by lamplight. Far on the edges of my hearing, on the rim of consciousness almost, came the long, wavering ululation of a wolf. There it was again, echoing faintly against the far shore of the lake. Then suddenly, there was a closer call of much lower pitch; two animals confirming their relationship to each other and the land.

The printed page, which had occupied me so completely, vanished. The yellow sphere of lamplight and the logs that confined it fled. There were only the stars, the mountains, and the stillness and the great, swelling dark beyond.

October 5, 1989

I did something I would not have thought possible. I put on approximately three-quarters of the roofing, all in one day.

Amazingly, the day, though dull, stayed windless. Sheet after sheet went up. I finished the last screws when it was too dark to see; the metal became very cold to lean against after the sun went down and my head was ringing from all the bashing of nails required to make the starter holes for the screws. I put a dab of roof seal on each one as I placed it, just in case. The roofing is a few inches short of covering the main part of the cabin, but what a relief that it is on.

And now I am due out again. I am meeting lighthouse-keeper friends in the Bella Coola Valley; they have to be lifted off by helicopter and their trips outside are rarer than mine — if I miss this chance I might not see them again for years. In any case, a trip down there is imperative to pick up my stoves. I took some parts for them to a welder in the valley last July. He faithfully promised to have them done and shipped up to Nimpo by the next mail day. The same thing happened each time I went out, but he still has not finished them. I have told him that this is the ultimatum as next month the lakes start to freeze; if Richard does not bring the stoves in before freeze-up, I will have to do without them until after Christmas. I can see that I'm going to be doing a lot of interior work during the early part of winter and it will be miserable to attempt it without heat in the cabin. If the welder still has not completed the stoves I will bring them to someone near Nimpo to finish — I now know a welder who lives there and wish I'd been aware of him before.

CHAPTER 24

October 26, 1989

It is useless to ask a wandering man
Advice on the construction of a house:
The work will never come to completion.
                                                — Chinese Book of Odes

I shouldn't have done it. But when my light-keeper friends asked me
to go back with them to Ivory Island, on the fishboat that was taking
them home, then get a ride part way back on the Coast Guard helicopter,
how could I turn down such an opportunity? It would use up only three
or four extra days I thought and, after all, the roof was almost complete.

I have been associated with Bella Coola for a number of years
now, but the road ends at the town and I had never been west of it.
A gaggle of fishboats cluster by the wharf, but the piece of water in
which they sit is surrounded by precipitous mountains and looks
more like a lake; in fact the water itself is so lacking in salt that little
traditional seashore life is evident. Were it not for the slight tide that
creeps in and out over a patch of mudflats, it would be hard to believe that it was the sea at all.

It took a day and a half in an old fish packer to reach Ivory Island
and the open sea. The island was a naturalist's delight; even though

I could walk around its rough and untracked edges in a day, I con-tinually found new treasures within the deep, moss-drowned coastal forest of its interior and the vastly different and fascinating intertidal zones. I had plenty of opportunity for exploration for the "couple of days" stretched into several as, for one reason or another, space on a helicopter was not available. So it was nearly two weeks after my arrival that I climbed into an old, twenty-seater monster and was transported over shaggy islands and the white-spumed fangs of rocks to another light station, which was only a short boat ride from Bella Bella; I had to charter a plane from there back to Bella Coola. It was a spectacular flight. The tops of the six-thousand-foot mountains, which we barely cleared, were dusted with fresh snow; their walls swooped steeply down to the long, grey inlet winding far below.

There was new snow, too, on the mountains that separated me from my home. But I decided to chance the shorter summer route over Maydoe Pass and down the big rock slide to Sam's cabin — I figured I could always turn back if the pass was too difficult.

There was bare ground underfoot until I reached Top Lake but the steep wall ahead of me, bisected by the black slash of a creek, was white and forbidding and soon lost in the cloud. I have no sense of direction but reckoned that if I kept above the tree line, I should be able to find the way. I had left Rimarko at the crack of dawn, but as the days were so short, the sun, whose vague position was just dis-cernible by a yellowish glow in the fog, was already well past its zenith and I knew I did not have a lot of daylight left.

Up I started, soon sinking into deep holes in the snow, the poor dog struggling miserably and resignedly behind. The fog closed around us.

It is the western side of the pass that is most difficult, for to avoid the worst of the bluffs and bush, it is necessary to maintain elevation for quite a way. Which is perfectly easy when you can see where you are going. But the country is steep and broken into gul-lies. Nor was the tree line much help, for tongues of balsam fir stretch up and down the mountain there; looming in the fog, separate from other topographical features, they were all totally unrecognizable. After a while, I was no longer sure I was still heading in the right direction; I might even be doubling back down into Maydoe Creek. I kept a small wind at the back of my neck, slightly towards my right ear, but there was no guarantee the wind direction would be constant; it was bound to eddy and swirl around the land masses.

A covey of ptarmigan erupted, a brief flutter of birds as white as the snow. I found myself following a trickle of water that I knew I had never seen before. The walking was easy there, a shallow basin, so I followed it for a while. Apart from the muffled creaking of my feet in the wet snow, it was very quiet. Then I heard a little tinkling sound, which, in a few minutes, proved to be the trickle of water, happily launching itself into space down a sheer rock face, where there was no chance of me voluntarily following. But the mist did eddy sufficiently for me to make out what could only be a portion of Banana Lake far below, so at least I knew I was on the right side of the mountain.

It was a long, wet, slippery struggle to find a way around the bluff and down towards the lake. I missed the big rock slide and my trail so I fell, slithered, scrambled, and fought my way through sodden underbrush which grew wetter as I lost height. I remembered that on my first trip through this way, the bush had become less dense closer to the lake and looked forward to reaching more open ground. But I was further north than I had been before and the bad brush went right to the water's edge. It was horrible stuff to try and travel through. I was saturated anyway and the water was fairly shallow by the shore, so into it I went, wading for what seemed miles, occasionally climbing onto the rocks where the water was deeper. At last I reached the easier part. From then on, although the light was all but gone and I was unutterably weary, it was just a question of putting one foot in front of the other until Sam's cabin loomed in the dark.

Bob and Francie had been there since my last visit. They had patched the larger holes, the bear had made, put fresh plastic over the window holes and replenished the woodpile on the porch. The bear had broken the lamp's chimney, so its flame was feeble and smoky, but the cabin was warm and dry, and that was all that mattered.

I've been home almost two days and still have not managed to force myself back to work. It is snowing wetly; an inch is plastered stickily

to everything visible within the short radius of the lamp's light outside the window. Sometimes the wind stirs a flurry of white flakes
that whisper momentarily against the glass.

November 1, 1989

After the roof was finished, it seemed that the first thing it would be
expedient to tackle would be the porch floor. The impending winter
made it imperative to have storage space under cover. The porch
floor was not as simple as that of the first cabin, for it included steps
from both the future walkway and the ground on the north side of
the cabin. This, coupled with the extremely uneven ground at this
location, meant a lot of fiddling and hunting for bits and pieces, the
whole job taking a couple of days.

The attic floor is to be made of store-bought boards (although I
had to cut my own two-by-fours to support them) but when I came
to lay the insulation, I found that the packets of styrofoam contained sheets only one-inch thick, instead of two as I'd thought. I
have put them in, but will wait to lay the boards until I see how
much fibreglass is left after I have done the walls; perhaps I can put
some of the latter up there.

However, I had to bring the boards inside. It was much easier to
drag them through the big gap of the gable end rather than a window hole so most of them are now in a pile in the attic and a few lie
temporarily over the styrofoam as a platform from which to work.

The gable ends are next; the south one is to have two windows
in it, the north one both a window and a door. The framing for
them, their supports, and the door itself have still to be found and
made.

The weather both drags me back and spurs me on. It is unstable
with a mixture of rain and slushy snow, which makes me desperate to
get the work done and my materials under cover, but the gloom and
chill and endless winds are hopelessly depressing. My joints ache
and I move as slowly as if the air had turned to molasses. Will there
ever be an end to this dreary torture?

November 3, 1989

When I was out, I discovered the reason for the smoke that plagued me last September. The local mill at Nimpo had burned down. Some locals were accused at first, for not everyone welcomes the mill, but then an electrical fault was discovered. The mill was over thirty miles away and I find it hard to believe that it should have given me such thick, dense smoke. The air currents must have been just right.

I have not yet properly digested all the mail I received at the end of my Ivory Island adventure. A large part of it is a result of an article about the building of my first cabin that I wrote for *Harrowsmith* magazine.

Because my camera was broken, the magazine asked me for diagrams of the single-handed log-raising operations (they had subtitled the article "Log-building for the Single Woman!"). I subsequently submitted them but was amused to see that their artist had "tidied" the drawings and made all the logs pencil-straight, with correspondingly regular trees growing behind them. I felt it did not convey at all what I had to deal with, but honest drawings, complete with every twist and wriggle, would perhaps be too confusing.

It was *Harrowsmith*'s idea to put the name and address of my proposed hiking business at the end of the article and, in the mailbox, there was a deluge of letters addressed to: *The Nuk Tessli Alpine Experience.* I never came up with a better name than Nuk Tessli, and in fact I have grown to like it. (It has come to my notice, however, that some of the local people at Nimpo Lake have decided on a different name for the place since I have occupied it — Spinster Lake.)

I was amazed at the variety of reasons that had inspired people to write. There was a rash of "How brave!" and "How courageous!", which is flattering but ridiculous, and there were even a few "Especially for a woman!", which does not even deserve the dignity of a comment. For some people, I was paralleling their own experiences — many of these writers were now retired and living in more convenient situations, but loving the times when they, too, had the freedom. Another section of people wanted "tips on building log houses." I am far from capable of giving much advice, for the bulk of my decisions are so specific to my particular situation that few of them would be applicable elsewhere. Techniques, for those who need them, can be found in a multitude of books and courses. When a person asks me, "What skills will I need?" and "Please tell me what not to do," I know he or she will be much happier living at the edge of a rural town where help, expertise, and companionship are available. Skills will always find a way of arriving, it is attitude that is important. If you think you can do something, it will happen. I can live this way because, even during my blackest moments, I have never doubted that I can do it; life in a city, which is unfamiliar and unnatural to me, would defeat me before I even began.

Many letters touched on the myth of living close to the land. There is no myth, simply an awareness of the way the land works. That can be learned by anyone — fortunately I acquired most of that understanding during my childhood. City-bred people with food, shelter, and entertainment provided by someone else, and an education that perpetuates both the desirability of the industrial dollar and the remoteness of the land, have well-cemented concepts to overcome. One New York correspondent expressed a desire to "live the way the natives used to before the white men came." He then decried modern native carvers for using chain saws to rough out their totem poles. He did not realize that firstly the peak of carving skills came only after the white man's metal blade was introduced — and secondly, before the chain saw, all the roughing out, the drudgery, was done by slaves. Would this New Yorker, in his desire to live as the natives used to, raid other tribes to obtain menials for his boring work? Or would he himself be a slave?

When I was in the Anahim Lake store on my last trip out, a woman with a laden shopping cart in the next aisle suddenly screeched to a halt and backtracked, then said delightedly over the oranges, "Are you the lady in *Harrowsmith*?" At which I naturally glowed, but then the woman's expression changed to one of perplexity and eventual bewilderment. "But what," she said, casting her eyes at the store, the groceries, and me, "but what are you doing HERE?" When I told her that I had to eat like everyone else, she scuttled off in such wordless horror, I can only assume that I have totally shattered her delusions about wilderness living. She must have assumed I could thrive on nothing but cloudberries and nectar of the gods. I surmise she must have been one of the new residents who came into the area because of the mill; no local person would think that way.

I need food, shelter, companionship, mental stimulation, and toilet paper, just the same as anyone else. The only way in which my life might differ from that of a city person is the time frame. I am not geared to the watch and the grids under the glossy pictures of a wall calendar, but to the sun, the seasons, and the proportion of daylight that it takes me to cover a certain piece of ground: a *sinik* the Greenland Eskimos call the latter. The distance a *sinik* entails varies tremendously depending on the type of country travelled, daylight length, even the urgency of the journey. After all, it was not so very long ago that everyone on this continent lived in a similar way. The push-button generation seems to have already forgotten its origins.

November 5, 1989

Last year, on this same date, my brother had a birthday party for his house, which was the same one that we grew up in, and which was a hundred years old. My little cabin is still not completed and the big one is barely begun. I wonder if there will be any sign of either of them in a hundred years?

CHAPTER 25

November 13, 1989

I have been home two and a half weeks since the Ivory Island expedition, but progress seems infinitesimal. I creep about like a snail; it is all I can do to drag myself around, let alone the materials that I must work with. I am lucky if I get a total of four or five hours work done in a day. The current run of storms are much to blame for this. The wind howls and moans, beating my body with raw gusts of air when I am out in it, and my mind when I attempt to relax. I have tried wearing the ear protectors indoors, but although the storms are muted by them, they are so distorted that I think some roaring doom is about to descend on me. The shutters are up permanently in the little cabin and this adds to the gloom. We've had days of torrential rain when the sky was so dark it was almost frightening; Noah is the only one who could view such weather with equanimity. Then there were two days of fine, horizontal snow which accumulated sufficiently on the ground to allow me to shovel it around the walls. The little cabin, which had been cold while the wind could howl beneath the floor, became instantly warmer, but that night it poured with rain again in a roaring deluge and washed both the snow cover and all the banking clean away. Provincial news on the radio is full of floods and washouts in the lower mainland; near Bella

Bella, a whole village had to be evacuated.

I never seem to be very good at measuring and, despite a considerable amount of effort at the time, the floor joists of the new cabin sloped down towards the waterfront. If I wanted a level floor I would have to build up the joists with wedges six-inches high and twenty-two-feet long. This meant every floorboard had to be dragged out and stacked on the porch. With some difficulty, I found a beetle-killed tree in the swamp that had a section of trunk more or less straight for twenty-two feet. The long, thin triangles that eventually emerged were too heavy to drag in whole, even though at that time there was a good covering of snow on the ground to ease their passage. The wedges had to be cut in half, which meant nine hauling journeys in all, the extra one being for the saw.

As the wedges and the hand-sawn floorboards had many small discrepancies, each one needed endless fiddling with and adjusting. Also, the boards all had to be edged — this occupation is designed to catch a saw operator right in the small of the back so that at times I had to rest whole minutes before I could straighten up again. I had already laid some of the boards when it occurred to me that it would be far easier to put the fibreglass around the root cellar before I covered it. I spent a day finding offcuts of boards to line it — there were many rocks to fit them around — but then realized I did not know if I was going to have enough fibreglass. I had collected all the sawdust that I could, but this was to be a much bigger root cellar than the other and would require a lot more commercial insulation. The house walls were more important at this stage.

And when the basement was walled and boarded in, I would not be able to get into any of the crawl space unless I designed another trapdoor, extra to the one over the root cellar, to give me access. So I now have one in the kitchen area, right next to where the stove will go. Crawl space is an apt name, for the boulders and foundation supports make a fair obstacle course of it, but it will give me some storage area for things like wire and stovepipes and trimmings off the roofing, stuff that is unsightly and bulky, but that is worth hanging on to, just in case it comes in handy one day.

If I was employed by anyone else to do this, I would have given up long ago. The only thing that keeps me going is the knowledge that eventually an end must come. Someday I will sit and dream and do whatever takes my fancy and not feel guilty about it or consider it wasted time. Someday.

November 21, 1989

Having a floor meant I could now put in the stoves. In Bella Coola, by standing over the welder, I finally got him to finish them.

There are two stoves. One is a barrel stove that had been half buried in a bank and used in a fish-smoker. It has two extremely heavy cast iron ends on legs that are designed to sandwich the body of a forty-five-gallon drum between them. One end sports a door and the words, "CORDWOOD. Coast Foundary Ltd.: Vancouver BC," the other an aperture for a square, obsolete chimney which I had the welder adapt to fit a standard, round eight-inch pipe.

This makes an excellent heater, but I also needed a cook-stove that would have a top with removable lids and a good-sized firebox. I had a door and the stove top (which I had used at the camp) and had asked the welder to make a box to fit them. Because the stove top was heavy and already at home, I did not fly it out, as I obviously should have done, but merely described how I wanted it fitted and gave him the exact measurements. He had obviously not under-stood my requirements; the hole he had cut for the stove top was as much as a half inch out at one end. The top does not fit into the hole as it is supposed to, but sits awkwardly over it at one end and, unless I prop it up, sinks in at the other. I don't know anything about welding but I am sure it is possi-ble to cut cast iron more accurately than that.

The cookstove has a six-inch chimney hole; in Bella Coola I had bought both six- and eight-inch pipes, dampers, and elbows, a T-junction, and an adapter. However, while I was visiting in the valley, ordering half a beef from the man who sells me his potatoes (the potatoes have come on the last plane and the meat will be fro-zen and flown in after Christmas), I was presented with a stovepipe oven. This is simply a double-skinned drum that fits into a chimney, the smoke and heat travelling between the two layers of metal. It has a six-inch pipe, which means it fits the cookstove; with the two sizes of pipe and only a limited amount of room between the floor and the ceiling, it has been quite a jigsaw puzzle to put it all together.

I lit the barrel stove at once. The cabin is still a windowless, uninsulated shell with a line of daylight in between each filler. Despite their original tight fit they have already shrunk considerably. The wall section under the porch, through which I have been dragging all my materials, is still wide open. But now, when my hands become numb, I can creep to the stove for warmth.

The next job was to carry inside every single board, two-by-four, and pole, including the large stack of tongue-and-groove lumber that would be used to line the walls. It had not received the shelter of the porch, there being no room, and was encrusted with frozen snow. Some of the bales of insulation had been outside most of the summer; one had a hole in its plastic cover so now there was a solid block of ice in the bottom. I opened it and put it closest to the stove. My new floor was instantly cluttered.

Next the windows were fitted into their holes, first the ones in the west walls to keep the snow from blowing in. The final section of wall under the porch was completed and I made a door to hang in the door hole. (I like hanging doors; there is a peculiar satisfaction in making it fit and swing effortlessly. I can play at opening and closing it for hours.)

With every gap that was blocked, the power of the stove could more readily be felt. One day, I thought to try the little firebox stove and found that the hole in the top was not the only inaccurate piece of work. The door had been so badly hung that it would close only with force, whence its top still strained outwards and let in far too much air. The welder had had the door, so there was no excuse at all for this. A lump of solder behind the hinge was the problem; the only tool with which I could attack it was a piece of chain saw file which had to be broken into a two-inch length to fit into the space available. Eventually the obstruction was ground down and the door now shuts properly. More wasted time. The stovepipe oven heated in about half a minute to 700°F, if the gauge is anything to go by, so looks as though that part of it is going to work very well.

Finally the insulation went up. Even the sun deigned to shine on that occasion, a little weak and wintry, but it was there. It rises so far to the south now that it first appears to the right of the hump that forms Louise O'Murphy's shoulders. The light that came into the cabin was much filtered by the years of dirt that covered the window panes, but it was wonderfully cheering. Its reflection on the wind-rippled water, as I had long anticipated, flickered and danced over my ceiling.

It seems incredible, but in three days I must leave yet again. Next weekend is the Bella Coola Christmas Craft Fair, which I cannot miss because the publishers of my first book, *To Stalk the Oomingmak*, have promised me that the book will be ready for it; I only hope the postal system will be equal to their efforts.

CHAPTER 26

December 21, 1989

The solstice. Sun has beaten dark. Whatever happens now, the days are growing longer.

The lake froze over during my last trip out. After November's depressing gloom I had almost dreaded coming back for these three weeks of even shorter days before Christmas, but in fact, they have been quite pleasant. I would have wished for less cloud and colder temperatures to consolidate the lake, but the weather has been far less turbulent and the solstice has come with a rush. When the sun shines in the morning, it illuminates the cabin with a soft, orange glow and, as it climbs higher, it sends the long shadows of Stump Island fanning out over the ice towards me. Sometimes the wind drives whirling snow devils down the lake; the sun and shadows play with these and make interesting patterns. I have chopped a waterhole close to the wharf and the snow around it stays permanently marked, but the tracks that lead out onto the ice, where I make occasional, cautious forays, are rapidly blown away. Although there appears to be three or four inches of ice wherever I test it, there is a lot of overflow which saps my courage when I feel it subsiding beneath my feet. I think there might be open water still in the middle of the lake, but I haven't investigated very far in that direction.

The Arctic book is beyond my wildest dreams. I had visualized a cheap little volume on paper little better than newsprint as is so often produced these days. But this book can only be described as elegant. It is a small coffee-table book, hard cover, with one of my watercolour Arctic skies on the dust jacket. It is as much a drawn journal as a written one and illustrations adorn every page.

I had expected that the way I felt about the Arctic would have been diluted, even changed a little by the publisher's choice and arrangement of the piles of material I had sent her. But, if anything, the integrity of what I was trying to depict was enhanced; I could not have wished for a better-looking book. And yet, as with the magazine articles, once it was in print, even though I knew it so well I could quote chunks of it by heart, it seemed as though it was not done by me at all. This was mine, and yet not mine; me and yet not me. I wonder if other authors feel this way?

My trip out last month was probably the fastest I will ever do along the river, for I walked from Sam's cabin to Rimarko, a distance of perhaps thirty miles, in only nine hours. The weather was dry and frosty, the swamps were frozen hard, and I simply flew. The river crossings, however, were none too pleasant. The recent rain had raised the level of the water to spring levels, which was crotch deep in the main channel. The crossing just below Sam's cabin, which had to be done before daylight, was the worst. The air temperature was, at a guess, -15°C. New shelves of ice had spread from the banks during the night and rafts of slush ice tinkled and whispered between them, glinting eerily in the moonlight. I had thought the moon might give sufficient illumination for the crossing; however, its feeble beams could not light up the bottom of the river — I would have to cross from memory. The thought of sitting naked in the snow and sliding into the river (for the bank was steep just there) was not too tempting, but the longer I stood looking at it, the worse it would be; so in I went. My weight broke through the ice beneath the bank, but I could not wade through it without laboriously chopping a channel. The river is only a couple of dozen paces wide, but the agony of those minutes was excruciating. The dog tore around in circles until she was warm; I was halfway round Banana Lake before feeling returned to my feet.

The break-ins at Sam's cabin have actually been very fortunate for me as they have shown me what a bear can do. I obviously cannot hope to keep a bear out downstairs should he really want to get in, so I am gambling on being able to make the attic of the big cabin bear proof. The boards for the gable ends are heavy and copiously nailed, and a solid trapdoor has been designed for the top of the attic ladder. A bear could probably rip these apart if he was standing on the ground, but the only way he can reach them is by climbing the posts that support the porch and I'm therefore presuming he will have at least three legs occupied in hanging on, and only one free to use as a pry bar. He could no doubt pierce the metal roofing with his claws but, should he be able to reach it (such as when the snow is deeper), I'm hoping the steepness and slipperiness will put him off. All being well, when the snow is that deep, the bears will be in bed.

The final trimmings of the attic, the lining of the walls and the door and window facings, were not essential jobs. But by doing them I have the enormous satisfaction of completely finishing the first room in either of the cabins. I can clean up the mess and survey the miraculous tidiness and emptiness. It won't stay that way once I start storing things in it, but after a year and a half of effort, that is quite a milestone.

I had been keeping one or other of the stoves going in the main room of the big cabin and they, combined with the bits of sun that came in through the windows, seem to have dried the wall insulation, even the wettest pieces that I put behind the heater. The cottonwood boards I bought from Williams Lake were low grade to begin with and they have warped and split considerably due to their treatment during the year. They were difficult to fit; they are also quite damp and will therefore shrink.

The little chain saw is now out of commission — the sprocket on the bar has siezed up — so I have had to use the big saw for some of the carpentry work — not a very happy situation. Its kickback is so great it is dangerous in confined spaces and it belches forth a lot of blue smoke; I wasted an hour replacing all the diaphragms in the carburettor and playing with the controls, but if anything else I have made it worse. Still, I now have an L-shaped corner seat under the south and east windows, and some of the cupboards and shelving are started. My remaining nails will have to be carefully husbanded; even so, I will not have enough. I once entertained a hope that I would move into this cabin before Christmas, but that is obviously not going to happen now.

Barbie and Alex have invited me to Rimarko for the celebration and Gloria and Roger have asked me to join their family at Wilderness Rim. But I feel a bit awkward barging in at their particular family time, so have planned to arrive at Rimarko on the 26th of December and Nimpo on the 27th. That way I will enjoy everybody's company and have plenty of Christmas goodies, without feeling I am imposing too much. It means leaving here on the 24th and spending Christmas Day on the trail.

December 28, 1989

I am writing this in Gloria and Roger's kitchen at Wilderness Rim. The clock ticks on the end wall of the room, the fridge hums, the tap drips, and the little blue figures on the microwave oven read 5:24 AM. I have breakfasted already, but I expect it will be a while before anyone else stirs. Every nook and cranny in the place is occupied, for the Folsoms have four children, three of them with spouses, and five grandchildren.

The most unexpected Christmas present I received was on Christmas Day. The weather going out was lousy. There was a warm southwest storm and it even rained a little. Banana Lake was frozen but insecurely; the ice had been licked clean by the warm wind and was so slick that even if I had wanted to risk it I could not have stood up on it when the wind gusts came. Most of the travelling had to be done on the rocks around the edge.

The swamps which had been so firm and fast on the November trip were as soggy as ever. Many of the holes were innocently covered with snow and were not apparent until I fell into them. My snowpacks were soon saturated; I could feel water squelch between my toes.

Bob and Francie had not started trapping so the low, log frame near the mouth of the river was tentless and covered in snow. Buddy

Jones's cabin was some distance further on. I knew it would be locked, but thought I might use the woodshed for shelter as I had no tent. My Christmas dinner would be a packet of soup and a couple of pilot biscuits. "This is your choice," I kept telling myself. "This is your choice."

It was growing dark as I came out of the forest and could look over the frozen flats to the lake. Because it is so much bigger, Charlotte Lake is always open later than any other in the area. Just beyond the flats was a boat. It was perhaps half a mile away. A fisherman? Surely none of the summer people were about. "If only I could get a ride," I thought; but even as I watched it, I heard the motor start and the boat pulled away round a point out of sight.

On I plodded over the frozen flats until I eventually came around the point myself. The boat was a few yards distant, pulled into shore. In it were Bob Cohen; Cornwall, Barbie's son; and another youth. Bob and Francie had been invited to have Christmas dinner with Barbie, and Bob, knowing both my intended arrival time and guessing where I would probably spend the night, had gone up the lake especially to meet me. If I had made better time and had headed straight for Rimarko, I would have cut off the peninsula on which the Jones's cabin was situated, but in that case, I would have encountered a message in a can tied to a tree, at a place where the trail runs by the lake, telling me to expect a ride sooner or later. Bob had been going to wait at the river mouth until dark; he had been there only twenty minutes when he saw me emerge from the bush.

Lonesome was into the boat way ahead of me, pack and all. The boat is a beautifully made freight canoe which has more recently acquired a fibreglass skin. It was calm in the river mouth, but out on the lake, an ordinary small boat could not have handled the boisterous wind and solid walls of water that reared up over the gunwales and dumped all over us. Bob was worse affected, being in the stern and having to look where he was going. He wore a hat trimmed with bits of fox fur and, by the end of the journey, it was difficult to say who looked more like a drowned rat, him or the dog.

Barbie's brother-in-law and his family of six were staying at Rimarko, so the little house was pretty crowded. The children were excited about their toys and Ainslie was full of a new bunch of kittens, all of which were remarkable in some way or another. Everyone had waited Christmas dinner for me; the contrast between that and the prospect of Buddy Jones's woodshed could not have been greater — or more welcome.

Chapter 27 ·

March 5, 1990

It is so quiet here. And the snow is so clean. There is no snarl of traffic, no stink of fumes, no electric hums and beeps and irritating radio noises. I was in Buenos Aires for a week once, waiting for necessary papers to travel to the Falkland Islands. I often sat in the little court-yard of the boarding house in which I was staying. It was surrounded by walls of multi-storey apartment houses. Sounds of cooking came from one window, opera singing from another, traffic from the road beyond the walls. It was only then that I realized most people will spend their whole lives never knowing what it is to live without human noise. It was like a revelation to me, for, having experienced it so often it had never occurred to me that other people might not have done so. These people, and probably the majority in today's world, will never know the beauty of silence. And if they were presented with it, it is likely that the first thing they would do would be to destroy it.

How much easier it is to unload a plane that stands on a solid sur-face, without having to swing everything over a gap of water. The pilot who came in yesterday was a stranger, a man Richard had hired

for the winter; as he stepped from the aircraft, which was parked close to the wharf, he looked up at the big cabin and said, "But it's beautiful!" He was the first person to give me any praise for the place and his spontaneity meant far more than the words themselves. I thought it looked beautiful, too, particularly now that the junk and debris were hidden beneath four feet of smooth, impeccable snow.

There is a lot of work still to do in the interior of the bigger cabin before it is habitable. The kitchen area will be the most complicated for the shelving has to be arranged in an L and also has to accommodate a window. Some of the poles to support the shelving still have to be hunted up in the bush.

There are just enough leftover wall boards to build two partitions, one to form an alcove near the door for coats (with a space underneath for the dog to sleep — I am afraid she is pretty much an inside dog these days) and the other to more or less divide the west wall in half for a short distance, giving me a lot more interior space for shelves.

However, at the moment, although the sun has long since risen, I am trapped in the little cabin. I am canning meat. The bulk of the last plane load was the half beef I bought in the Bella Coola Valley in the fall. It had been cut up into half a dozen lumps; larger and they might have been a problem to handle, smaller and they would run a greater risk of spoilage if the temperature became too warm.

I could, I suppose, attempt to find my own wild meat, but the steer in Bella Coola has been reared on a small farm and has not suffered the trauma (and consequent loss of quality and flavour) of being shipped to an abattoir. Home-canned meat in a jar can be frozen and thawed indefinitely without damage to either itself or the container so it will not need to be stored in the root cellar. I hope it will last me at least two years. Close to the big cabin is a fallen tree that has made a cave in the snow. This, sealed with snow, should keep the unprocessed meat well frozen until I want to deal with it.

People are sometimes worried by the idea of home-canned meat, but its doubtful reputation derives from the old water-bath canners. If a pressure canner is used, and if the instructions are followed properly, there can be no mistake. My Atnarko neighbour has eaten home-canned meat for the whole sixty years of her life and is certainly none the worse for it.

Time and pressure are the keys to adequate preservation. Because of my altitude, I must increase the latter by five pounds per square inch. The canner has a rocking valve which hisses when the pressure is correct. As I have a woodstove and it is not possible to exactly control the heat of the flames, I must sit within earshot to make sure the pressure does not drop.

So although the sun is high and shining on the blue-striped snow, I am still confined to the little cabin, all doors and windows wide open, while the stove roars and the canner hisses. Even though I cut the meat by lamplight this morning, half the day will be gone before I can start on my shelving. The sun will be flooding through the windows in the other cabin, marking spring pathways over the floor in a way that has never happened before. This time last year, there was not a vestige of a building and very little disturbance there. My snowshoe track to the waterhole followed the rim of the hollow, and the only other marks were, for a few brief hours, the little peppery mass of the springtails, as they followed their destiny on the billowy smoothness of the snow.

March 12, 1990

All of the interior of the big cabin that I can do at present is finished; the floors are swept and scrubbed, even the window panes are clean and shining. The insides of the windows lack facings as I don't have any boards left with which to make them, so ragged bits of fibreglass are visible around the window frames, but that is a job that can be done later. One corner of the cabin is full of offcuts of bits of wood and there are no shelves in there yet; neither has the area under the work table, which will store art materials, been properly partitioned. They will all have to wait.

Suddenly, almost without warning, I am ready to move in. Tomorrow is the big day. It would have been wonderful to have everything completed right down to the last detail, but I don't suppose that anyone who has built their own house has ever totally finished it before inhabiting it. This one will be a vast improvement on the condition of the other two cabins that I occupied; the little one on this place was first slept in on the night of the big windstorm, and I was forced into the one at the Atnarko because the grizzlies were suddenly around at the advent of the salmon-spawning season. That cabin did not even have a floor, and only half a roof. Moving into this one is going to be a real luxury.

March 14, 1990

The new cabin is gorged with sunshine. The windows are wide open and a small, fresh breeze filters into the light-filled room. Rectangles of pale gold drape, Salvador Dali-like, over the newly filled bookcase, the ornaments on top of it, the bright, woven blanket on the bed, the hand-stitched rugs my mother made, and the tawny, scrubbed-wood floor. All those months, years even, of dreaming and planning and working are finally coalescing into reality.

But it will still be a long time before I can sit back and enjoy it. There is much to be done before I leave in two weeks time to go tree-planting. Everything must be brought over from the other cabin. A large stack of lumber must be milled to provide boards for the walkway, the deck, and the wharf, all of which will have to be built when the snow goes. Three dead white-barks lean over the lake and, by falling them onto the ice and cutting them up there, I can keep most of the debris from littering the land. Falling trees is not the problem it was last year for the snow is of a completely different consistency. By tramping around the trees in the afternoon, when the snow is soft, I have a solidly frozen platform from which to work the following morning.

Canning the meat is a priority — I reckon another six batches will finish it. There is one hissing away right now, which is why I don't feel too guilty sprawling on my bench and enjoying the brilliant sunshine. I must also apply myself to the fat textbook for the industrial first aid course I plan on taking in Williams Lake before tree-planting this year. Up here, knowledge of hypothermia would have been more appropriate than what to do for cyanide poisoning, but the course will give me the basic knowledge to deal as best as I can with most emergencies. This is especially important to know if tourists are to come here. I have yet to receive any positive replies since the enquiries after the *Harrowsmith* article.

I now have the radiophone I had hoped for. It is not yet legal for, as with everything else, the paperwork is taking forever to go back and forth. It has two aerials; these have to be erected. But when the paperwork comes through I will be licensed to operate a "coast, land, space, or earth" station. So, all you Martians, start broadcasting; I'm ready for you.

March 15, 1990

I have had visitors — Bob, Francie, and Patrick, of course: no one else would be up here this time of year. They have come into the country to pick up the supplies they have not used, rather than leave them to the depredations of the bear. When Francie saw the attic of the bigger cabin, she asked if she could bring some of the bulkier boxes to be stored there, to save them the labour of having to transport them all home.

I was only too pleased to be able to do something for Bob and Francie as the taking up to now has been all one-sided. I would no doubt find ways and means of dealing with this country if they weren't here, but there is no denying that their tents and cabins and their

freely given knowledge has made life a lot easier for me. Not everyone is so generous towards an outsider who is horning in on their
own private domain.

At one time, hunters were the only tourists for whom Bob and
Francie catered. But now summer sightseers are an increasing part
of their business. Bob gave me some advice. "You have to be a bit
careful with bear stories," he reflected as he chewed a sumptuous
lump of beef. "At one time, when a grizzly hunter got et, it was
good for business. But with trail riders and hikers, that's bad news.
They might be scared away."

March 25, 1990

There is a *Peromyscus maniculatus alpinus (var. nuk tesslii?)* in my
new house. I wondered how long it would take the little beggars to
occupy it. I hear this one creeping about in the insulation behind my
head as I sleep. It often makes a peculiar snoring noise, a sound that
is common here, but that is very unlike anything I ever associated
with a mouse in other parts of the world. I shall have to resort to
Warfarin. I hate the idea, but I cannot keep ahead of them with traps
when I go away. If I let them be, the fibreglass insulation in the walls
will soon become a disaster area.

I had quite a trouble finding any Warfarin; the city mice in
Williams Lake are apparently immune to it. But I did not want anything more potent and eventually I tracked some down in an
old-fashioned hardware store. The shop assistant looked at it. "No
tax for murder," she said as she rang it through the till.

March 27, 1990

I have to be in Williams Lake
by Monday morning, April 2,
to begin the first aid course. I
have made another pilgrimage
to Snowshoe Mountain. How
different the snow is this year.

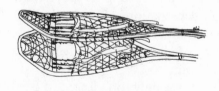

I could walk on the lake without snowshoes almost as soon as I
arrived at the beginning of the month and, although I had no broken trail beyond the bluff, going up the mountain, the snow was

wind-packed and firm. Above the tree line, I stuck the snowshoes on their tails in a drift and climbed to the top without them. They looked like two willow leaves with all the flesh gone and only the veins left, as if they had lain beneath the snow all winter.

It was so warm on top, I did not need my coat. The sky was blue and the dazzling curve of the Coast Range swung about me. In places where the snow had lain thin on the rocks, it had turned to wafers of ice as clear as glass which I crunched like candy. The tiny pair of dots that were the snowshoes were the only alien thing visible. Quotation marks at the beginning of a sentence with no end.

Someday I will be able to stay here for the spring. I will watch the first patches of ground appear, brown and resinous with their litter of needles, on sunny slopes beneath dense-canopied trees. The lake will become snowless and grey and the air bubbles trapped in the ice will grow and mesh together until they form a network of vertical crystals that are no longer safe to walk on. Candling, they call it. The sun and wind will break the ice, the crystals will fall in tinkling masses, and the waves will push and pile them on the shore. The lake will be alive again.

I will have to batten down the place for bears and bugs before I leave. I am roasting the remains of the meat at the moment. There was not enough left to warrant another batch of canning, so the dog and I will eat it on the way out.

A light, sun-filled snow has started to fall. The slight breeze is driving it exactly against the corner of the cabin so that it whirls past the windows on both sides of the seat. Slouching, as I am, I cannot see the shore of the lake, only the unmarked white of the ice and the windblown islands set into it. It is if I am in a ship, sailing through a sea of snow-filled light, with silent spume flying past my bows.

CHAPTER 28

Date uncertain, but close to the end of June 1990

Quiet. A small wind, grey sky, the tick of occasional spits of rain on the roof. Warblers sing. There is a soft flutter of the fire in the stove. The grey water below the window laps. A pair of loons fish in the quivering channel. Peace.

It has been a traumatic three months. I fell through the ice on the way out; I successfully wrote my first exam in twenty years; it has been the wettest and, for me, the most miserable tree-planting season to date; and, out of the blue, a fairy godmother waved a magic wand and wafted me to Toronto to the National Magazine Awards, which culminated in an interview with Peter Gzowski for CBC Radio's "Morningside." And I have received my first deposit for the Nuk Tessli Alpine Experience.

I went through the ice just above the confluence. In years gone by, Bob and Francie shoved a pile of brush into the river at a narrow point and this formed a functional snow bridge. Last year, beavers built a couple of dams just below the confluence, flooding the place where the snow bridge had been and drowning it.

The ice on the new beaver pond did not look very good. I tested it with the axe; it was only two inches thick and, being a hot, sunny afternoon, the top inch was slush. Still, my snowshoes appeared to be holding me. I had taken the bindings off and had my boots through the toe pieces only. My gear was on the toboggan and I tied an extra long string to it to spread our respective weights as much as possible. The dog, as usual, was told to stay on the bank until I was over — she is becoming used to river crossings. Chop and shuffle, chop and shuffle. I almost made it but did not test the last two steps — and in I went. Whether it was the snowshoes that resisted my descent or my mind that clicked into overdrive, I don't know, but I appeared to sink quite slowly. I had time to wonder how far down I was going to go. The river under the snow bridge had been very shallow, but I had no way of knowing what was under the beaver pond at this point.

I stopped when the water reached the bottom of my shirt pockets. The dog thought it was some new game for with an incredulously delighted expression, she started to prance around my head.

My next immediate thought was the snowshoes. But they had come free from my feet and floated up to the surface. I threw those back to the toboggan and crawled out. It was only after I was partially dry that I realized I might just as well have continued across the river, but once out of the water I had no desire to go back in it again.

Suprisingly, I felt immediately warm, wet clothes and all (I was wearing pure wool to the skin this time). I did not want to change my clothes until all the river crossings were finished. The binoculars unfortunately had another ducking, but they seemed to be none the worse for it this time. I found a shadier spot and the ice there held me, but remembering how Sam's cabin crossing had collapsed right after I had gone over it last year, I went over with great apprehension. However, I am pleased to relate there were no further problems.

Instead of going out via Rimarko — the road would be undrivable and I had not left my truck there — I crossed Charlotte Lake to the rash of summer cabins on the north side. When the lake is frozen it is a much more direct route to Nimpo. Charlotte Lake is the only lake in this area where pressure ridges of any size occur. On that trip I encountered them at their most spectacular. There were some cutting through the middle of the lake, but most occurred along the shore and around all the little rocks and islands. Jagged teeth of ice holding head-sized boulders were thrust ten vertical feet into the air. To add to the spectacle, the lake ice was grey already, but the ragged giant tombstones were still pure white. Traces of old snow machine tracks could be seen; their violent displacement was evidence of the drastic shifting and buckling that the ice had undergone. The groaning, pinging, and tearing noises were extraordinary and continuous — my own lake is comparatively silent and I assume that is because of the snow on it. It was interesting to think that this is how the earth behaves on a much larger scale. Despite the obvious drama of the ice, I assumed the movements would be slow enough to be unnoticeable to humans, but that is not always the case. A friend told me she was once looking at the lake when she saw the three-foot-thick ice undulate like water when a stone is thrown into it. All of a sudden, there was a huge bang and the whole lot was flung into the air. I had to cross the pressure ridges occasionally. They were rough enough to climb quite easily, but it was a real chore manhandling the toboggan over them and there was often an open lead of water on one side of them.

At Nimpo, there was a phone message to call the *Harrowsmith* editor. This was not too unusual so I had no inkling of what was to come. I was informed that I was one of six nominees for the Personal Journalism category of the National Magazine Awards, which were to be held in the Sheraton Hotel in Toronto at the end of April. Was I coming?

I had never heard of the magazine awards; as for going to Toronto, well, wouldn't it be nice, but I was flat broke and would not have a cent until I started tree-planting. Two days later, while I was in Williams Lake wrestling with the physiological difference between freshwater and saltwater drowning, the editor phoned me and told me that my fare would be paid.

The glitter of the banquet and award ceremony and the ostentatious extravagance of the big hotel itself were enjoyable enough. But I somehow could not whip up the passionate enthusiasm that was obviously affecting quite a number of the thousand people who were in the room, and which I felt I should show to demonstrate how much I appreciated being there. I suppose it was because the whole situation was so far removed from anything I had experienced before, that I had no parameters as to how to react. Music is merely a collection of sounds until you have learned to enjoy it. Stone age peoples from hidden valleys, when put into planes, show no emotion whatsoever, whereas I, who have no trouble understanding the principle of flight, am a gibbering lunatic. A friend of mine took up parachute jumping. She told me that it was not the first jump that was traumatic, but the second; it was only then that she knew what to expect.

I didn't get my award, but I was in good company, because Pierre Berton and Margaret Atwood didn't get theirs either.

I first started writing to an anonymous public by sending letters to Peter Gzowski's "Morningside" on CBC Radio. I had just built the Atnarko cabin and the letters described my experiences there. The euphoria after the first one was read induced me to unburden my soul to Peter Gzowski once a month whenever I went out for mail. These letters have since been expanded into *Cabin at Singing River* which Camden House has undertaken to publish and for which Peter Gzowski has very kindly written the introduction. It was Camden House who phoned Peter Gzowski and told him I was going to be in Toronto.

If the National Magazine Awards had seemed unreal, it was nothing compared with what went on in the CBC building.

To begin with, the elaborate security was a little unexpected. When I asked a uniformed man where the door was (for it had been skilfully hidden), he took one look at my backpack and said disdainfully, "This is the CBC building!" and was about to order me onto the street. I explained why I was there and he crossly asked me where was my badge? Nobody told me about any badge.

That little matter taken care of, I next presented myself, name and host stuck prominently to my clothes, at the receptionist's desk. And this is where I first experienced the almost fanatical devotion that all the CBC personnel have regarding time. "But Peter," said the receptionist, aghast, "is busy right now. He won't be available for twenty minutes!"

I was only too pleased to have that little space in time so that I could get a bit of the feeling for this extremely foreign environment.

I was shown a bench that would not have held more than two persons; obviously the place did not cater to idlers. People looked at me curiously as they walked past. (Someone sitting?) In a few moments, a lady in spiked heels with very long legs and a very short skirt came striding up. "I'm Peter Gzowski's producer," she said, shaking my hand. Then, that same perplexed look, "But Peter is in conference and will be busy for another twelve and a half minutes! Would you like a drink?"

"What I would really like," I replied, "is a washroom. The bus station is having extensive renovations and I could not find one there."

"So would I!" stated the producer. Away went those staccato heels, clattering on the bare stone steps of the building, with me shambling sneaker-footed behind. There, the producer did not waste a second. She already knew quite a bit about me, but she kept up a rapid fire of questions. So there I was, sitting on the can, having a conversation with a CBC producer, similarly employed in the next cubicle.

The old studios in Toronto are extraordinary places. Everything — walls, ceilings, floors, tables, chairs, microphones — is painted matte black. What a dreary and depressing environment in which to spend one's time. I can understand that surfaces could not be shiny as that would affect the acoustics, but would colour make any difference?

The studio is divided into two by a thick, glass wall; on the side away from the interview area is a barrage of control panels which would put the set of a Star Wars movie to shame. Open doors along the corridor had revealed several other identical rooms. The place was a veritable Watership Down.

Suddenly, Peter stood in the doorway. "I don't want to talk to you before we are on the air," he said. "It will reduce the spontaneity of the conversation." So I trotted in and sat down; my voice level was tested and we were away. The producer had warned me that the item would start with a recording of the first paragraph I ever wrote to Morningside, read by Lorna Jackson, who apparently has delivered all my letters. She had told me it was to last fifty-four seconds. Not "close to a minute," but "fifty-four seconds."

"I live twenty-five miles from a road and seventy-five miles from a store in the heart of British Columbia's Coast Range. I built my house with logs cut from the forest...." The only lights that I could see were a narrow one directed to illuminate Peter's page and the green, digital figures of a tiny clock by his hand. At the fifty-four-second mark

exactly, Lorna Jackson finished and Peter smoothly started his introduction. Then he turned to me.

I enjoyed that interview. I suppose Peter's lifetime of experience
at putting nervous and naive people at ease had a lot to do with that.
He asked me all the usual questions — "Aren't you frightened being
alone? What if you get sick? You mean you actually bake your own
bread?" And because I am asked these things so often, I had no
trouble in coming up with answers. I was at first a little disappointed
about the banality of the queries, but when I later spoke to a friend
about the interview, she said, "The thing I most like about Peter
Gzowski is that he always asks exactly what I want to know." That,
no doubt, is one of the main reasons for his success.

The interview lasted fifteen minutes (my time, in other words,
approximately). I was out on the sidewalk so fast that only a very
fancy bit of footwork enabled me to rescue my backpack from where
I had left it behind the receptionist's desk. The producer was shaking one hand and thrusting a subway token into the other. ("Don't
you use money?" I asked. "Yes," replied the producer, "but a token
is quicker.") I, however, preferred to walk; it was only two miles to
the friend's apartment where I was staying. I felt completely spun
around; the rhythm of walking would make my thoughts my own
again.

A clock on a building indicated it was twenty past twelve. Including the twenty-minute waiting time, I had been in the CBC
building for less than three-quarters of an hour.

And therein lies the only major difference between my life and
anyone elses. At home, three-quarters of an hour is hardly time to
say hullo. In Toronto, it constituted a complete episode of my life.

July 2, 1990 (confirmed: I heard it on the radio)

Tree-planting is an itinerant occupation based on the conditions of
the moment and it is often difficult to have a reliable forwarding
address for mail. So in mid June, I phoned Gloria at Nimpo and
asked her to ship the several weeks' accumulation to me on the bus;
a deposit cheque for the Nuk Tessli Alpine Experience fell out of an
envelope while my mud-stiff rags were being dealt with at the
laundromat. The cheque was for three people for a full week's hiking. They did so hope that I could "fit them in" between the 7th

and 13th of August as that was the only time they had. Fit them in! I should say so. It was all I could do to stop doing a jig on top of the washing machines. This extra cash meant no more tree-planting for the season — I was going home. How often in the mud and rain had I thought about the trapezoids of sunlight travelling over the book-case and the floor (for in my mind, when I am away, the sun is always shining at home).

Not all my mail was so welcome, though. The permission for the extension of my property and the addition of a wharf had come through from the Land Office — along with a bill for $200 for the extension paperwork, $250 rent for the two square yards of wharf — it had to be a separate lease because it was on the water — an extra $150 for the paperwork for it, and the requirement for evidence of a separate insurance policy, which was to be, the insurance company informed me, another $500, because my two-yard-square wharf had to be classified as an airport. I had to fill in the answers to:

"How many runways do you have?"

"Where are your fuel dumps in relationship to the public who might use the airport?"

"How many pilots do you employ?"

"What provisions have you made to keep the public off your runways?" To this last, a friend to whom I showed the form replied, "Put up *No Swimming* notices."

Then there was the letter from the Williams Lake regional district council saying that the extension would require my property to be re-zoned as a recreational lease, a process which would take six months and cost $700. Fortunately, that was dropped when I was able to show that the original proposal for the licence of occupation had not been altered.

The last thing I did before I came home was to have a book-signing for *To Stalk the Oomingmak* in Williams Lake. I had never seen a book-signing, let alone been the instigator of one. It was in a supermarket and the bookstore manager squeezed an extra table in a corner for me, half blocking an aisle near the eggs. She had warned me to dress warmly because the blast from the refrigerator would prove quite chilly. I figured it would help with the arctic atmosphere.

Williams Lake is a mill and cowboy town and not exactly a mecca for literature. I can hardly blame the harrassed parents, weighed down with groceries and festooned with fretful children, being more irritated than anything, if they noticed me at all, when they had to manoeuvre their shopping carts around my obstruction in the aisle. I sat there with a frozen smile that had little to do with the blast of arctic air around my ankles. "You have to talk to people," said the bookstore manager, a most bouncy and personable woman. She only had to stand there for someone to stop and become interested.

I sold five books — one of them only because I belatedly phoned the only person I know in town and she phoned a friend of hers who bought it. Nonetheless, the store manager was quite enthusiastic about my "big sales." Apparently, the last person who sat through a book-signing there sold two.

At Nimpo, there was a message for me to phone a Nick Mason in Vancouver. I had never heard of him (although he claimed to have met me when we were teenagers) but I knew other relatives of his very well. It seemed he had just spent five months in Brazil and was on his way back to England, hoping to visit my place en route. Having to deal with yet another human being was the last thing I wanted to do just then, but I could hardly refuse him. I told him that if he could reach Nimpo in twenty-four hours, I would wait for him and he could hike in with me. I did not tell him that, for the first five miles of the trail up as far as Cowboy Lake, I expected him to help me portage a canoe.

CHAPTER 29

July 4, 1990

Barbie and Alex are leaving. How adamantly they had protested when they first arrived that they would never return to the city, but now they are going back. Admittedly, Barbie's kids are very creative and cannot receive the kind of education they are used to in the mail; unless Barbie wants to be separated from them for most of the year, she will have to move, too. Also, the caretaker's job pays no wages and it is expensive to live at the ranch. But for all their protestations, I think there are aspects of city life that Barbie and Alex also miss, although they probably don't admit it, even to themselves. Francie and I will be sorry to see them leave for they have been good neighbours. (I am not so sure about Bob: I think he has felt a bit outnumbered at times.)

Nick did more than his fair share of portaging the canoe — once he had it on his shoulders, he was unwilling to relinquish it — and certainly made that job a very easy one for me. It was not a full-sized canoe, being a little plastic shell weighing perhaps forty pounds. I paid very little for it; its bow was split and mended with wire, but it will save me over an hour's walk and will eliminate that horrible Big Swamp at the head of Cowboy Lake.

The little canoe was never designed for two adults (neither of us small) and two heavy packs. Needless to say, there was no room at all for the dog. She had to find her own way and spent most of her time in the water which slowed us up considerably.

The first little lake was full of yellow pond lilies just coming into bloom. At its head there was a beaver lodge. An animal snarled at us from inside it, but I think it was an otter. The portage from that little lake to the next one proved quite rough and I will not bother to bring the boat below it again. We had no sooner loaded our gear and ourselves, and wobbled precariously away from the bank on the second lake, when Nick looked at his watch and said, "Six o'clock. Time for supper." As I never use a watch, it would never have occurred to me to stop when the sun was still so high in the sky. However, figuring he was probably quite tired, I acquiesced.

It rained a little in the night, but the morning was sunny and very still, which was fortunate as any kind of wind or chop would have seriously affected our overloaded progress up the lake. It was a very pretty canoe ride by rocky promontories, islands, and through several narrow passages in the lake. But, what with one thing and another, we were much later than we might have been when we reached Top Lake.

Although the winter had been so lacking in snow, the extremely late spring had encouraged what there was to remain. There was far more above the tree line than I had yet seen at this time of year. Long, icy slabs filled every depression, covering perhaps half the ground. But the tardiness of the season had produced a wonderful flush of early flowers. Starry carpets of eight-petalled avens nodded in the wind; mountain marigolds and snow buttercups choked the runoff creeks; the pink balls of the moss campions and arctic louseworts vied for attention. And there was the little alp lily, considerable areas of it, blooming by crystalline patches of late snow. I was in raptures; Nick and the dog, however, seemed less enthused although they were only too pleased to be relieved of their packs every time I grovelled on the ground to take a photograph.

Poor Nick! It is natural for a man, no matter how "liberated" he is, to think that if a woman can do something physical, then it can't be too strenuous for him. But like anything, it is not strength that is

required in travelling through this type of country, but a condition-
ing of the muscles and brain. Nick was no longer bounding ahead
with enthusiasm as he had done, rather like a dog when first let out
of doors, at the beginning of the trip. In fact, he looked decidedly
miserable. He was cold, too, for his physiology was still geared to
the tropics; he had not slept well and he was now exhausted. The
sun did not stay with us and gradually, as we came round the skirts
of the half-way mountain, the Coast Range to the west became swallowed in gloom. As we plodded up the Horse Trail by Wolf Basin, it
started to rain.

Just before we dropped down among the trees, we were privi-
leged to see three cariboo, two magnificent-looking bulls and a
younger male who tagged on behind, suffering several horn tosses
in his direction if he got too close. I was most excited and kept
telling Nick how lucky he was, but he didn't look as though he
thought luck favoured him right then.

He was no longer even attempting to be civil when we eventually reached Nuk Tessli, but how quickly the smiles returned when
he was sitting down, in dry clothes, enveloped by the heat of the
stove and drinking a mug of tea. Fortunately he is a good-natured
soul and his equilibrium was soon restored. It is a good job that I
have friends on whom to practise my tourist-guiding skills; I will
have to be careful not to push paying guests too far beyond their
capabilities.

At Nimpo, there has been a reshuffling of the float plane bases. The Stewarts still operate out of their lodge as Tweedsmuir Airservice, but Richard has left and sold out to a man from Quesnel, who is no longer going to run the business during the winter. Floyd Vaughn, however, the man who brought my supplies in the first winter I was here and who used to fly into Lonesome Lake, has now started up his own business with his wife. I have known Floyd and Lora so long that it seems like old times to do business with them again.

So it was Floyd who came in this morning with a load of tongue-and-groove lumber and took Nick back out to Nimpo Lake. The weather has continued windy and rainy, even sleeting and hailing, since Nick has been with me, and he never saw the country at its best. "Come again," I said as I shook hands with him on the wharf. "Send you friends. Bring your orchestra!" (For he plays bass in a classical orchestra in London, England.)

He climbed aboard and I pushed the wing out from the wharf, turning the plane towards the channel between the islands. The motor leapt into life, the gulf between us widened, then with a roar, the plane was in the air and gone. A loon quavered, squirrels chattered; then silence.

I listened to it.

Waves lapped, the little birds sang, the river, summer-full, roared distantly across the lake.

I was alone for the first time in three months.

It was wonderful.

July 5, 1990

I have just over two weeks before my first official guests arrive. These are not the group of women hikers whose cheque I received in the laundromat, but a couple I met when I first arrived in Canada, eleven years ago. I warned them that things might not be quite ready for them, but I wanted the place to look as well as it could before they arrived.

The interior of the little cabin — which can now receive its proper title of "guest cabin" — was the most important job. It needed a complete renovation; the kitchen shelving was the only thing that could be retained. The counter and table had to be dismantled and stored on the porch; the bed being merely planks on log rounds was easy to toss outside. First, the walls. Some of the fibreglass had been blown out of the cracks between the logs and I had to replace it and make it fit, and nail laths over the insulation to both hide it and keep it in place. That this was a fiddly job due to the unevenness of my logs goes without saying. Then I turned over and properly fitted the floorboards. Some had shrunk so much there was a gap of an inch or more between them. Once in place, I coated them with Varathane; the boards from the big, kinked tree in front of the cabin are sixteen-inches wide and look very fine.

Next came the kitchen counter, followed by an L-shaped seating bench, long enough on each side for a sleeping body, and some of the shelving. The corner behind the stove will eventually hold more shelves, but I don't have the lumber for that at the moment.

The windows, including the fixed ones, all had to be taken out of their holes and scraped of what vestiges of paint they had left. Most of the putty was either missing or very brittle and was replaced. The frames were painted Signal Red. (I have to write that in capital letters as it is such a bright colour. But it adds exactly the right accent to the yellow log walls.) The outhouse seat received the same treatment. The hummingbirds are mad about it. The structure for this esoteric building was a work of art as the big rocks that sandwiched the hole had to be catered to. I would love to live in a house with rocks incorporated into the walls that way, but in this climate it is not practical.

That done, I became Octopus Woman. The junk in the attic was turfed out and I began to line the gable ends and the ceiling with the boards that Floyd had brought in. I sat on the floor and held them under the rafters with feet, knees, hips, elbows, or head, whatever was appropriate, to leave my hands free to bang in the nails.

Whenever I find myself with a spare hour I work on the Big Clean-up. No one will have any idea as to the amount of time and effort this job is taking. I cannot hope to finish all of it but if I pile the most obvious brush in as inconspicuous a place as possible, and rake the ground free of debris, it should look fairly tidy. The mess in the swamp will have to stay put but fortunately few of my guests are likely to walk far into it. There are a lot of naturally fallen trees there and by hiding stumps and shoving the cut ends of brush out of sight it will be hard to distinguish my mess from theirs. I also want to brush out a trail to the lookout bluff. I have found a longer, but much easier route up there; however windfalls and eye-poking branches still make it tiring.

Then there is the walkway and the deck to be surfaced with the boards I cut in March.

I'd better get a move on.

July 16, 1990

The sun! The sun! For two whole consecutive days! That is the first time that has happened since I was in Ontario. And the sky is absolutely cloudless, so it looks as though today is going to be just as glorious.

I could not resist launching the canoe as the smoke from my breakfast fire, suffused with orange from the rising sun, wafted over the lake. Golden mist curled through the sun's shaft on the water, then burned away and the bush was diamond-fresh and a-sparkle with dew. How breathlessly quiet it was, only the soft plop and bubble of the paddle and the occasional suprisingly clumsy crashings of the dog. I wish Nick could have seen the place like this. But perhaps he never could, even in the same conditions. For I look at it all with a mind shaped by the life I have led and he would look at it with his. Obviously, few people can feel the same way about the wilderness as I do, or they would not be living in a city. Nick's passion is classical music, which I enjoy but can never hope to equal him in either knowledge or delight. The natural world is my symphony. Each flower, each leaf, each rock and bird and insect is a note; every unusual harmony is exciting, every familiar strain like coming home.

CHAPTER 30

July 20, 1990

I finished everything that I wanted to do with moments to spare. The place looked perfect. I wasn't exactly sure which day my friends were due but reckoned that I might even have had a day to spare. However, I had just cleaned up the last of the mess by the new deck, when a plane circled around a few times then landed and taxied in between the islands. It was not Floyd's regular plane, but he often hires other pilots and planes in the summer. As it came closer, I could see there were three passenger heads silhouetted against the windows of the plane, instead of the two I had expected. Assuming my friends had brought an extra person with them, it was not until I grabbed the wing and eased the plane against the logs, that I realized that all the occupants, pilot included, were complete strangers. "We read about you in *Harrowsmith* and heard you on Peter Gzowski," said the pilot, "and thought we would drop in for a visit."

To say that I was flabbergasted would have been an understatement. When Camden House accepted *Cabin at Singing River*, the publisher said to me, "You realize that the world will beat a path to your door." But never in my wildest dreams did I imagine this.

Rudy, the pilot, and Fern, his wife, intimated that they would like to return for a longer stay in the future. But this time, after tea, they climbed back into the plane and flew home to Vancouver.

To me, Vancouver is practically at the end of the world. In the most ideal of conditions, it takes me a minimum of three days to get there, although, if I chose, I could fly to Nimpo and catch the daily scheduled plane down from Anahim, arriving almost as quickly as my visitors. But when I go to the city I have so much business to do en route, and so much stuff to haul, I have to go by road. I shall never, as Rudy and Fern have done, treat the journey between us as a Sunday afternoon drive.

And people think I'm isolated.

EPILOGUE

If there be
A heaven on earth
It is this
It is this
It is this
        — Persian inscription

I am doing something that I have dreamed of for close on five years. It is the picture that I have kept in my mind throughout all my trials and tribulations; it is the one thing that has kept me going. I am sitting on my deck in the morning sunshine.

When I first saw the place, after the two-and-a-half-day hike from the Atnarko, I slept at the edge of the swamp fairly close to where my building camp was situated. There was a hard frost that morning and it was uncomfortably cold. As the sun rose I walked across the point to catch the warmth. And I thought: "This is where I want to be." It was only a fleeting thought, for at that stage I hardly imagined that I would be given the claim, let alone go through with the project.

I still find it hard to grasp that it is all real. My first guests took one look at the place and said, "How on earth did you do it?" Looking at it all, as a complete entity seen through their eyes, I can hardly believe it myself. It was like the hike two years ago in forty-below weather: it was accomplished one step at a time.

I never want to do anything like this again. Three cabins in eight years. A friend of mine has just had her second child; since the first one was conceived, her every thought and action, waking or sleeping, was involved directly or indirectly with the needs of her children, a situation, I am sure, with which most young mothers are familiar. The cabins have been like that with me; and, like a parent, I will be involved with them to a greater or lesser degree for a long time to come. I still have quite a lot to do even before the initial labour is finished and there will never be a complete end to the work, but the pressure is off. None of it is urgent any more. I can sit, sometimes, and relax. The sun warms me, the lake, the river, and the small wind sing to me, and I am content.

As I look back in my journals, to the day when I was waiting for the first plane to land, I find these words. "All I have to do is tell the pilot to take it straight back out again and I will not lose a lot, just a bit of time and cash — and a certain amount of face." But I would have lost more than it is possible to measure. I would have lost everything.

July 27, 1990: Nuk Tessli.

Chris Czajkowski, (pronounced Tchaikovsky, like the composer), was born and grew up on the edge of a village in the north of England. Natural history always fascinated her, and she trained in agriculture, specifically the dairying industry. Once qualified, she travelled to Uganda where she taught at a farm school for a year. Chris then travelled widely through Asia, before arriving in New Zealand. There she worked primarily on commercial diary farms and sheep stations. Chris spent her spare time exploring the beautiful scenery and discovering the flora and fauna of the region. It was in New Zealand that she first began to sell her watercolour paintings of the scenery and wildflowers.

After travelling through the South Pacific and South America, Chris emigrated to Canada. Attracted by the mountains of British Columbia, she eventually came to roost in an area of the Coast Range near Bella Coola, 300 miles north of Vancouver. She built a log house twenty-seven miles from the road and accessible only by foot and canoe. Through her letters to Peter Gzowski in the 1980's, she became a regular contributor to CBC's "Morningside" program. Her adventures during that time became the subject of her second book, *Cabin at Singing River* (Camden House, 1991).

Diary of a Wilderness Dweller is the story of her adventures building her second cabin, this time a mere twenty mile walk from a road. This cabin is located on a high-altitude, fly-in lake, from which she guides artists and naturalists on backpacking trips amidst the magnificent mountains that surround her. Living at such an altitude and so far from a road gives Chris a unique opportunity to study the wildlife in an area which has had so little documentation that much of it remains un-named.

Chris travels throughout British Columbia giving slide shows to local botanical and alpine garden clubs, libraries, and university audiences. She operates The Nuk Tessli Alpine Experience, an opportunity for artists, hikers and naturalists to discover the beauties of the Coast Range. She can be contacted by writing to The Nuk Tessli Alpine Experience, Nimpo Lake, British Columbia, V0L 1R0, Canada.

photograph by Joyce Dorey